DOROTHY E ZEMACH

writing

SENTENCES

THE BASICS OF WRITING

MACMILLAN

Contents

Introduction

To the teacher iv
To the student v

1 I go to an unusual school   6

- Basic parts of speech: nouns, pronouns, and verbs
- Definition of a sentence

2 Funny stories   14

- Basic parts of speech: prepositions, adjectives, and adverbs
- Reviewing the parts of speech

3 I'm from Bangkok   21

- Vocabulary to talk about your country and city
- Subject / verb agreement with the *be* verb
- Three sentence patterns with the *be* verb
- Adding details to a sentence with adverbs of time

4 She seems lonely   29

- Vocabulary to describe people and their feelings
- Sentence pattern for stative verbs (*seems, looks*)
- New sentence pattern for the *be* verb: *There is / There are*
- Expanding sentences with adverb phrases of location
  (*in the corner, at the back*)

5 She has brown eyes   37

- Vocabulary to describe animals and people
- Sentence pattern for the *have* verb
- Using *a* and *an*
- Describing people with *be* and *have*

6 I like playing soccer   44

- Vocabulary to talk about hobbies and interests
- Sentence pattern for action verbs
- Combining words with *and*, *or*, and *but*
- Using gerunds

7 Faded jeans are cool 52

- Vocabulary for describing clothing and fashion
- Subject and object pronouns
- Combining sentences with *and*, *but*, *or*, and *so*
- Putting two or three adjectives in the correct order

8 I'm a business major 60

- Vocabulary for school subjects
- The simple present and present progressive tenses
- Adverbs and expressions of frequency
- Format of a paragraph

9 I'm in Barcelona 68

- Irregular past tense verbs
- Sentences with indirect objects
- Format of a postcard and an email
- Formal and informal language
- Using questions and exclamations

10 It's a kind of French game 75

- Vocabulary to describe popular international items
- Passive sentences
- The topic sentence, supporting sentences, and the concluding sentence

11 It has great graphics 83

- Vocabulary to describe popular media
- Supporting sentences and concluding sentences
- Strengthening and weakening adjectives
- *Too* and *not ... enough*

12 I've never been to Australia 91

- Vocabulary for writing about travel and experiences
- The present perfect tense
- Contrasting the present perfect and the simple past
- Using *However* in a paragraph

Additional materials 98

- Key sentence patterns
- Verb patterns
- *Can*
- Common irregular verbs

To the Teacher

Writing is an important form of communication in day-to-day life, but it is especially important in high school and college. Indeed, almost all other subjects, from the social sciences to the hard sciences, require students to demonstrate their knowledge and opinions in writing.

Young adults who are beginning writers in a second language face the challenge of wishing to express sophisticated and relevant ideas with limited vocabulary and grammatical structures.

This new edition of *Writing Sentences* is designed to help beginning students express their ideas clearly and accurately by teaching the most common sentence patterns and verb tenses in English. Students read sample texts to discover the target structures, which are then summarized in clear charts. Students move from tightly controlled practices to freer exercises until they can successfully write accurate sentences. As the book progresses, students learn to link words, phrases, and then sentences to create longer texts.

Units are organized around an interesting theme to engage your students. Relevant vocabulary is used both in the model writing and the students' own writing. The structures and grammar are practiced in a variety of ways, and each sentence in every exercise is linked to the unit theme. Usually the sentences in an exercise form a cohesive text, so that students are working with the content of a paragraph (with a topic sentence and supporting ideas) even when they are focusing on individual sentences. Thus even sentence-level work on grammar guides students to becoming fluent writers in English. The final three units of the book specifically address paragraphs and introduce the concepts of topic sentences, supporting sentences, and concluding sentences.

Each unit ends with a writing activity that summarizes the material in the unit. Students combine the sentence patterns, vocabulary, and grammar they have learned in a creative, engaging task. The activities take students through the traditional writing process: They brainstorm ideas, organize them with the provided graphic organizers, write their texts, and then share them with other students and comment on one another's writing.

An appendix in the back of the book summarizes the sentence patterns, provides additional verb charts, and lists irregular past tense verb forms and participles for easy reference. The Teacher's Guide supports the instructor by offering teaching suggestions, a discussion of marking and grading writing, suggestions for writing journals, ideas for supplemental activities for each unit, and answers to exercises in the Student's Book.

Learning to write well takes practice and patience. Students need clear guidance and support, positive feedback, and interesting ideas to write about. I hope this book provides this for your students and that you enjoy teaching from it.

To the Student

Writing is a very important part of your school and university study. You explain your ideas and show your opinions in writing in almost every class you take. Clear writing helps you communicate clearly, and even helps you think clearly.

This new edition of *Writing Sentences* will help you write interesting, accurate sentences that express your ideas. You will study vocabulary, spelling, and grammar, and you will have many chances to practice what you learn. You will learn to write several sentences on the same topic in a unified paragraph. You can choose what to write about and what words to use, and you will even have the chance to "play" with language in a creative and enjoyable way.

As you progress though the course, you will have many chances to read example sentences and paragraphs from this book and from your classmates, and you will share your writing with them. You will learn how important the reader is to the writer, and how to express clearly and directly what you mean to communicate. I hope that what you learn in this course will help you throughout your academic studies and beyond.

You should come to your writing class every day with ideas and energy. Your instructor and classmates have much to share with you, and you have much to share with them. By asking questions, taking chances, trying new ways, and expressing your ideas in another language, you will add to your own world and the world of those around you. Good luck!

Dorothy E Zemach

I go to an unusual school

In this unit, you will ...
- learn and practice some basic parts of speech: nouns, pronouns, and verbs
- learn what a sentence is

This is not a grammar book; this is a writing book. However, if you know some basic grammar terms, you can learn how to write correct and interesting sentences more easily.

Nouns

A **noun** names something:
- a person or animal *(student, Ms. Clark, cats)*
- a place *(park, Taipei, classroom)*
- a thing *(chair, book, computers)*
- an idea *(love, education, friendship)*

Writers use nouns to identify what they are writing about.

1 Work with a partner. Look at the word web below. Add more nouns in the correct circles. Can you add more circles?

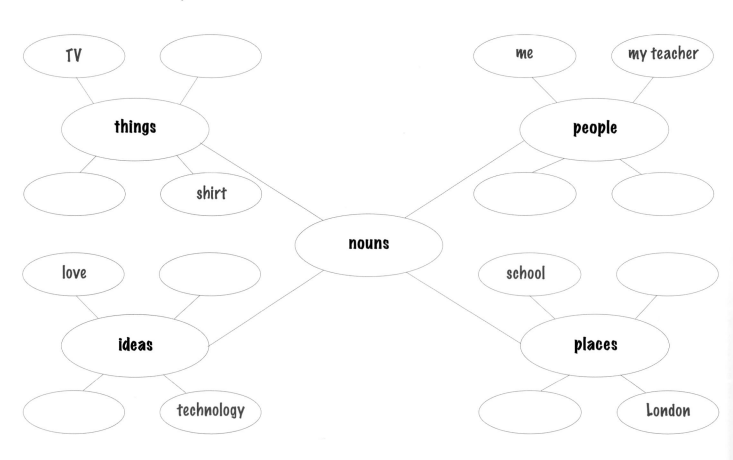

Pronouns

Pronouns *(I, you, she, it, them, there, etc.)* are words that replace nouns. They are used like nouns.

> *The **book** is difficult. (book = noun)*

> ***It** is difficult. (it = pronoun; means the same as book)*

Writers use pronouns so we do not need to use nouns again and again.

For example, the paragraph below is difficult to read and difficult to understand:

> *I go to an unusual high school in Vermont. The unusual high school in Vermont is for skiers. The other students and I take regular classes like math, English, and history. The other students and I also practice ski racing. The other students and I learn from our ski coaches. Our ski coaches teach the other students and me how to race faster. Our ski coaches train the other students and me hard. Studying and training at the same time is difficult, but the other students and I like studying and training at the same time.*

With pronouns, it's easier to read and understand:

> *I go to an unusual high school in Vermont. **It** is for skiers. The other students and I take regular classes like math, English, and history. **We** also practice ski racing. **We** learn from our ski coaches. **They** teach **us** how to race faster. **They** train **us** hard. Studying and training at the same time is difficult, but **we** like **it**.*

2 Look back at the second paragraph about the high school on page 7. What do the pronouns replace? Write the group of words.

a. **It** is for skiers.

It = *The unusual high school in Vermont* ....

b. **We** also practice ski racing.

We = ...

c. **They** teach **us** how to race faster.

They = ...

us = ...

d. Studying and training at the same time is difficult, but **we** like **it**.

we = ...

it = ...

3 Read the sentences. Write the second sentence again. Replace the <u>underlined</u> nouns with pronouns. Use the words in the box below. Each word is used once.

| her   his   ✓ it   she   them   they |

a. LaGuardia High School is in New York. <u>LaGuardia High School</u> is a special school.
It is a special school. ....

b. Students at LaGuardia High School want to be performers. <u>Students at LaGuardia High School</u> take classes in music, art, dance, or theater.

....

c. English, math, history, and science classes are also required at LaGuardia. All LaGuardia students must take <u>English, math, history, and science classes.</u>

....

d. Jennifer Aniston went to LaGuardia High School. Now <u>Jennifer Aniston</u> is a famous actress, and many people know <u>Jennifer Aniston</u>.

....

e. Al Pacino is another famous actor from LaGuardia High School. Have you seen one of <u>Al Pacino's</u> movies?

....

....

Jennifer Aniston   Al Pacino

Verbs

Writers use *verbs* to tell about the action in the sentence:

> He *studies*.
>
> They *played* soccer.
>
> She is *taking* a test.

or someone's condition or feeling:

> He *seems* bored.
>
> I *feel* happy.
>
> She *looks* worried.

See how the verbs change to match who does the action and when the action happens:

Who	I **play** soccer. Hamid **plays** soccer. My friends and I **play** soccer.
When	I **play** soccer every day. I am **playing** soccer now. Hamid **played** soccer yesterday. Maria **has played** professional soccer for six years. My friends and I **will play** soccer tomorrow. Our team **play** soccer last week.

4   **Read the story. <u>Underline</u> the verbs.**

> It <u>was</u> a beautiful spring day. Two university students skipped class and went to the park instead. They missed a test in class. The next day, they spoke to their teacher. "We wanted to come to class. Unfortunately, when we were driving to class, we got a flat tire. So we couldn't come to class. We are very sorry."
>
> "That is OK," their teacher said. "You can take the test now." The boys sat down, and the teacher gave them a piece of paper. "Here is the first question," she said.
>
> "Which tire was flat?"

Sentences

A sentence in English has a **subject** and a **verb**. The subject is a noun.

subject	verb
Students	**learn**.
The **students**	**learn** English.
The older **students**	**learn** computer science.
The **students** in our school	**learn** in the evening.
The best **students** in the school	usually **learn** quickly.

A sentence begins with a (capital letter) and ends with a (period):
The students in our class are learning English now.

It's important to know the subject and the verb in the sentence to make sure they **agree**:

- ✗ The student learn.
- ✓ The student learns.
- ✗ The students learns.
- ✓ The students learn.
- ✗ The students go to school yesterday.
- ✓ The students went to school yesterday.
- ✗ We had a test tomorrow.
- ✓ We will have a test tomorrow.

5 **Read the groups of words. Are they a sentence? Is there a subject and a verb? If yes, write the sentence again with a capital letter and a period. If no, cross them out.**

a. some schools are a lot of fun *Some schools are a lot of fun.*...

b. ~~for example clown school~~ ....

c. you learn how to make people laugh ....

d. for both children and adults ....

e. clowns take classes in acting ....

f. makeup, juggling, and making costumes ....

g. they also business classes ....

h. it isn't easy to be a clown ....

i. many clowns work in circuses ....

6 Read about Hometown, USA. In each sentence, <u>underline</u> the <u>subject</u> once and the <u>verb</u> twice.

> ___Hometown, USA___ ___is___ *a summer camp. This camp is in Minnesota. Children from many countries come there. They study English during the summer. The campers sing songs in English. They speak English to their friends. They play popular American sports. The food is American food. The campers learn a lot of English. They also learn a lot of American culture.*

7 Read the sentences. <u>Underline</u> the <u>subject</u> once and the <u>verb</u> twice. The verbs do not agree. Write the sentences again and change the verbs.

a. <u>American students</u> <u>can</u> <u>studies</u> a foreign language too.

American students can study a foreign language too.

b. One language camp teach Japanese.

....

c. Its name are *Mori no Ike*.

....

d. That mean "lake of the woods."

....

e. American high school students learns Japanese language and culture.

....

f. I wanted to go to *Mori no Ike* next summer.

....

g. Students from all over the U.S. comes to study there.

....

1

Marking nouns

Here are some words that often come before a noun:

a or an
the
this / that
these / those

- Use **an** before a vowel sound (a, e, i, o, u).

- Use **a** before words that start with consonant sounds (for example: b, d, k, m, s, t). Remember that in English, the consonant **h** is sometimes silent, so words like **hour** start with a vowel sound.

- **A**, **an**, **this**, and **that** are used before singular nouns.

- **These** and **those** are used before plural nouns.

- **The** is used before singular and plural nouns.

- An adjective can come between the noun marker and the noun:

    A large **school**   *This unusual* **school.**

8   Circle the correct word. Then <u>underline</u> the noun that comes after it.

a. My cousin is going to (a / an) <u>school</u> in Switzerland.

b. It's (a / an) hotel school.

c. (This / These) school teaches students about (the / those) hotel business.

d. It's (a / an) expensive school, but he likes it.

e. Two years ago, he went to (a / an) art school.

f. He didn't like (that / those) classes.

g. (This / These) days, he enjoys (a / the) classes at his school.

Spelling review

9   Look at these nouns and verbs about studying and learning. They are spelled incorrectly. Write them correctly.

nouns		verbs	
skool	*school*	lern	
clasroom		teatch	
studant		is studing	
techer		skiped	
Inglish		sed	
coash		trane	

Put it together: Sentence chains

a Work with a partner or small group. Look at the chart below. Add some more words.

●	✳	●	✳	●	✳	✳
The	crazy	coach	happily	kicked the ball	after school	again.
A	lazy	man	quickly	played the violin	in the classroom	all day.
This	sad	student	slowly	read a book	in the snow	at 6:00.
My	strange	teacher	carefully	sang a song	on the bus	in the morning.
Our	young	woman	loudly	told a joke	under the table	last week.

b On a separate piece of paper, each student writes a sentence with a group of words from each ■ column.

The man sang a song.

c Pass the paper to another student and read the paper passed to you. Write the sentence again, but add one group of words from a ✳ column.

The man loudly sang a song.

d Repeat three more times, until the sentence has a group of words from each column.

The crazy man loudly sang a song on the bus last week.

e 🔄 Share your favorite sentences with the class.

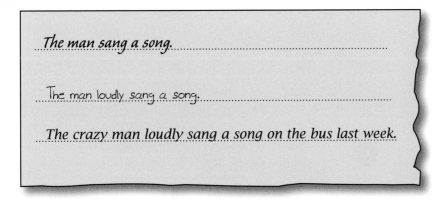

The man sang a song.

The man loudly sang a song.

The crazy man loudly sang a song on the bus last week.

2 Funny stories

In this unit, you will …

■ learn and practice more basic parts of speech: prepositions, adjectives, and adverbs

■ review the parts of speech

Writers use prepositions, adjectives, and adverbs to make their sentences longer. These words give more information about the subject and the verb.

Prepositions

Prepositions are short words (*at, on, for*) that connect ideas. They tell about time, location, or purpose (reason):

We eat dinner **at** seven o'clock.	time
My book is **on** the desk.	location
She bought a gift **for** her friend.	purpose

A **prepositional phrase** includes a **preposition** and a **noun**:

We eat dinner <u>**at** seven o'clock</u>.

My book is <u>**on** the desk</u>.

She bought a gift <u>**for** her friend</u>

Writers use prepositional phrases to give more information:

1 Work with a partner. Complete the story by writing the prepositional phrase from the box in the correct place.

✓down the street	in the afternoon	to the zoo
in his car	to the movies	to the zoo
		with this kangaroo

A man was walking ..*down the street*....... . Suddenly, he saw a kangaroo! He asked a police officer, "What should I do ?" ....

"Take him .... ," said the police officer.

"OK," said the man.

The police officer saw the man again .... The kangaroo was ....

"I told you to take the kangaroo .... !" said the surprised police officer.

"I did," said the man. "We had a wonderful time! Now I'm taking him ...."

2 Work with a partner. Write the story in exercise 1 again. Change the prepositional phrases if you can. Practice reading your new story a few times. Then read it to another pair.

....

....

....

....

....

....

Adjectives

An **adjective** gives more information about a noun. It answers the question *What kind of?* or *Which?*

   *The **red** cell phone is mine.*   [Which cell phone is yours?]

   *Her jacket is **leather**.*   [What kind of jacket does she have?]

Adjectives are important to writers because they help the reader to imagine or "see" what you are describing.

3   Read the sentences. <u>Underline</u> the adjectives. Then draw an arrow to show which noun or pronoun they describe.

   a.   On a <u>dark</u> night, a man was looking for something in the <u>tall</u> grass under a streetlight.

   b.   A young woman saw the man. She asked him, "Did you lose something?"

   c.   "Yes," said the man. I lost my new watch. It's gold."

   d.   "Oh," said the woman. "That's terrible. Where did you lose it?"

   e.   "Over there by that big tree," said the man.

   f.   The woman was surprised. "Then why are you looking over here?" she asked.

   g.   "Because it's too dark over there," said the man. "The light is great here."

4   Check (✓) the pictures that go with the story in exercise 3.

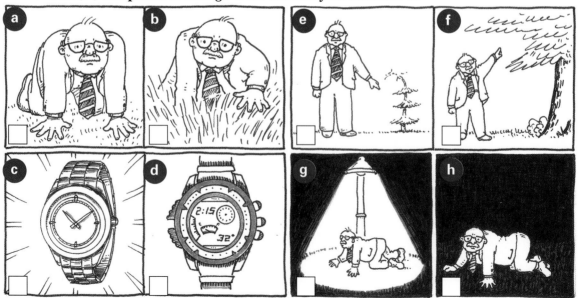

Adverbs

An **adverb** gives more information about the verb. It can answer the questions:

Where • When • How • For how long • How often • Why?

*It rained **yesterday**.*	[*When* did it rain?]
*She eats **slowly**.*	[*How* does she eat?]
*I **sometimes** play tennis.*	[*How often* do you play tennis?]

Writers use adverbs to tell their stories. Adverbs help readers imagine how events happened.

5 **Read the sentences from a story. Circle the verbs and <u>underline</u> the adverbs. Then draw an arrow to the verbs they describe.**

a. A new mother was walking slowly down the street.

b. "You are talking calmly and gently to your baby."

c. A man was watching the woman carefully. "Good for you," he said kindly.

d. "Oh, no," replied the woman sadly. "Her name is Anne. My name is Gloria."

e. The baby inside was crying loudly.

f. She was carefully pushing a stroller.

g. He looked at the baby and asked politely, "Is the baby's name Gloria?"

h. "Please, Gloria," said the woman quietly. "Relax. Don't cry, Gloria!"

6 **Now put the sentences in exercise 5 in order. Then write the story on a separate sheet of paper.**

The New Mother

A new mother was walking slowly down the street. She …

Recognizing parts of speech

Some parts of speech in English have special endings. Here are some examples:

nouns	verbs	adjectives	adverbs
~er, ~or teacher, doctor	is/are + ~ing is talking, is going	~y happy, funny	~ly happily, quickly
~ist scientist, chemist	~ed used, worked	~ive active	~ward forward, backward
~tion action, nation		~ic scientific, terrific	
~ment development, government		~ful useful, careful	

7 **Read the sentences. Circle the correct word.**

When Americans first sent astronauts up into space, they (discovered / discovery) that ballpoint pens did not (working / work). So, American (scientific / scientists) spent ten (years / yearly) and 12 billion dollars to (develop / development) a new pen. The (new / newly) pen could write upside down, under water, on (glass / glassy), and in temperatures from -5 to 300°C. The Russians (useful / used) a pencil.

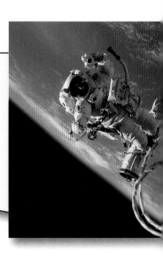

Spelling review

8 **Work with a partner. Circle the correct spelling for each word. Then write the words in the correct place in the chart.**

loudly / lowdly	replyed / replied	terrible / terible	usful / useful
offiser / officer	sceintist / scientist	their / thier	with / whith
quietly / quitely	seid / said	undre / under	youre / your

nouns	pronouns	verbs	prepositions	adjectives	adverbs
					loudly

Put it together: Grammar game pairwork

a You are going to play a grammar game! Work with a partner. Student A, stay on this page. Student B, go to page 20.

Student A

1 Look at the paragraph below. Some words are missing. Ask your partner to give you the missing words. Do NOT read the paragraph to your partner! Just ask for the words.

For example, say *Please tell me a noun.*

2 Write the noun that your partner tells you on the line.

3 When you are finished writing every word, read the paragraph to your partner.

4 Then your partner will ask you to give some parts of speech.

Have fun!

My Favorite Sport

My favorite sport is soccer. In England, it's called

_____ . It's a / an _____ sport to learn, and
  (noun)   (adjective)

it's _____ , too. You _____ soccer with a _____
  (adjective)   (verb)   (adjective)

white and black _____ . You also have to wear _____
      (noun)   (adjective)

shoes. You have to run _____ and kick _____ to be a
      (adverb)   (adverb)

good soccer _____ . I used to _____ soccer in high
     (noun)   (verb)

school. I wasn't a very _____ player at first, but later I was
        (adjective)

the _____ of the team!
  (noun)

Someday I hope to play as _____ as _____ .
       (adverb)   (noun: a person's name)

He / She _____ soccer on a / an _____ team.
     (verb)   (adjective)

b Share your funny stories with another pair of students.

Student B

(Student A, go to page 19.)

1 First, your partner will ask you for some parts of speech.

For example, your partner will say, *Please tell me a noun.* Say any noun that you want—for example, *cat, winter, dentist.*

2 Your partner will write your answers into a paragraph. When you are finished, your partner will read the paragraph to you.

3 Now, it's your turn. Look at the paragraph below. Some words are missing. Ask your partner to give you the missing words. Do NOT read the paragraph to your partner! Just ask for the words.

For example, say *Please tell me a noun that is a place.*

4 Write the place that your partner tells you on the line.

5 When you are finished writing every word, read the paragraph to your partner.

Have fun!

A Postcard from _____
(noun - a place)

Dear _____,
(your partner's name)

Hi! How are you? I'm having a _____ time on vacation. I'm
(adjective)

here with my _____ and my _____. Every day we go to
(noun)   (noun)

the _____ and _____. I'm taking _____ lessons, and
(noun)   (verb)   (noun)

now I can _____ very _____. For lunch, we go to a local
(verb)   (adverb)

_____ and eat delicious _____. Last night, we went to
(noun)   (noun – plural)

a / an _____ dance show. The dancers were all _____ and
(adjective)   (adjective)

they danced _____.
(adverb)

I'll see you _____.
(adverb)

Your friend,

_____
(your teacher's name)

---

b Share your funny stories with another pair of students.

3 *I'm from Bangkok*

In this unit, you will …

- ■ **learn some vocabulary to talk about your country and city**
- ■ **learn subject/verb agreement with the *be* verb**
- ■ **learn three sentence patterns with the *be* verb**
- ■ **learn how to add details to a sentence with adverbs of time**

| **Work with a partner. Look at the map of Thailand. Label the map with the words below.**

capital	mountains	northwest	river	southwest
coast	northeast	southeast	south	west

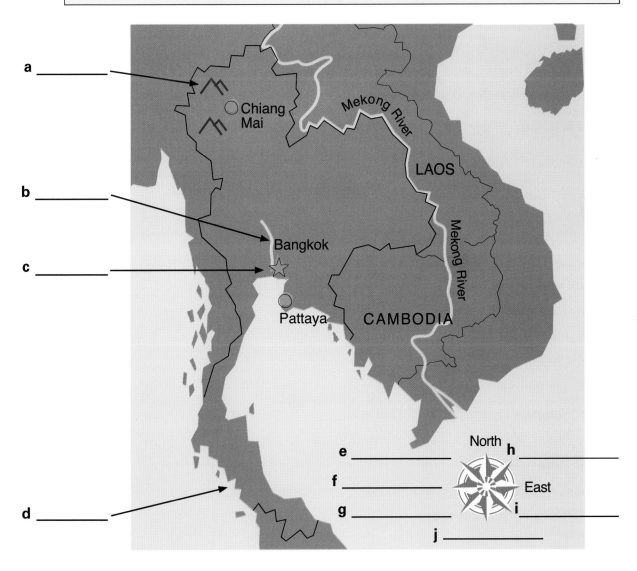

2 Work with a partner. Look at the pictures of Bangkok. Write a or b next to the words that describe the picture.

__ boring	__ busy	__ small
__ modern	__ international	__ crowded
__ exciting	__ rural	__ quiet
__ traditional	__ peaceful	__ colorful

3 Work with a partner. Read the sentences about Thailand and Bangkok. Circle T if the sentence is true. Circle F if the sentence is false.

a. Thailand is in Asia.   (T)   F

b. Bangkok is quiet.   T   F

c. Chiang Mai is a river.   T   F

d. Thailand is next to Cambodia.   T   F

e. Bangkok is the capital of Thailand.   T   F

f. Bangkok is both modern and traditional.   T   F

g. Pattaya is a city.   T   F

h. Chiang Mai is in the mountains.   T   F

i. The west coast is long.   T   F

j. Laos is northeast of Thailand.   T   F

The <u>be</u> verb

Look at the chart below.

subject (noun / pronoun)	verb	noun, adjective, or adverb phrase
I	am	Thai.
	am not	Chinese.
You	are	at home.
	are not	at work.
Mr. Martin He }	is is not	a teacher. a doctor.
Ms. Tagawa She }	is is not	in Chiang Mai. in the south.
My friends and I We }	are are not	at the beach. in the mountains.
The streets They }	are are not	noisy. quiet.

Note: In English, *you* can be used for one person or a group of people:
You are my teacher. (*you* = one person)
You are great students! (*you* = many people)

4 Fill in the blanks below with *am*, *is*, or *are*.

a. I .... from Chiang Mai.

b. Chiang Mai .... a city in the north of Thailand.

c. It .... not the capital, but it .... a large city.

d. It .... a modern city, and it .... popular with international tourists.

e. The weather .... nice, the people .... friendly, and the mountains .... beautiful.

f. I .... proud of my hometown, Chiang Mai.

Sentence patterns with the <u>be</u> verb

Most sentences with a *be* verb include something else after the verb.

- Some have a **noun** or **noun phrase**. These give another word that means the same thing as the subject. They answer the question *Who or what is (the subject)?*

    *Sunee is **my friend**.* (Who is Sunee?)

    *The Mekong is **a river**.* (What is the Mekong?)

- Some have an **adjective** or **adjective phrase**. These tell what the person or thing is like. They answer the question *What was (the subject) like?*

    *The mountains are **high**.* (What are the mountains like?)

    *Chiang Mai is **busy** and **exciting**.*

- Some have a **prepositional phrase** that gives a **location** (place). These answer the question *Where (is the subject)?* Sentences can have more than one prepositional phrase. These are adverb phrases.

    *Phuket is **on the coast**.* (Where is Phuket?)

    *Phuket is <u>**on the coast**</u> <u>of Thailand</u> <u>in Southeast Asia</u>.*
                1   2   3

5 Look back at exercise 3 on page 22. Copy the true sentences with the *be* verb into the right places here:

Followed by a noun:

a. ....

b. ....

Followed by an adjective:

c. ....

d. ....

Followed by a prepositional phrase (location):

e. ....

f. ....

6 Look at the false sentences on page 22. Change them to true sentences. Then compare your sentences with a partner.

a. *Bangkok is not quiet. Or, Bangkok is noisy.* ....

b. ....

c. ....

7 Complete the sentences about your country. Then read your sentences to a partner or small group.

a. I am from .... (*country*)

b. .... is the capital city.

c. My city is .... and ....

d. My city is not ....

e. The people are ....

3

Adding more information

Look at these sentences:

> *The weather is beautiful.*
> *The weather is beautiful **every day**.*
> *The weather is beautiful **in the spring**.*
> *The streets are quiet.*
> *The streets are quiet **now**.*
> *The streets are quiet **in the evening**.*

The second and third sentences in each group give more information by adding an adverb or adverb phrase of time.

8 **Unscramble the sentences. Add the correct form of the *be* verb. Put the adverbs and adverb phrases of time in the correct places.**

   a. The streets of Bangkok / in the morning / very busy

     The streets of Bangkok are very busy in the morning.

   b. The city / cold / in the winter

     ....

   c. after school / The children / noisy

     ....

   d. The restaurants / late at night / open

     ....

   e. excited / before the holidays / Many people

     ....

   f. in June and July / very rainy / Chiang Mai

     ....

9 **Look back at the last three sentences of exercise 7. Write the sentences again. Add some adverbs and adverb phrases of time. Then share your new sentences with a partner or small group.**

   a. ....

   b. ....

   c. ....

Spelling review

10 Write the words that describe the pictures. Then find them in the word search below.

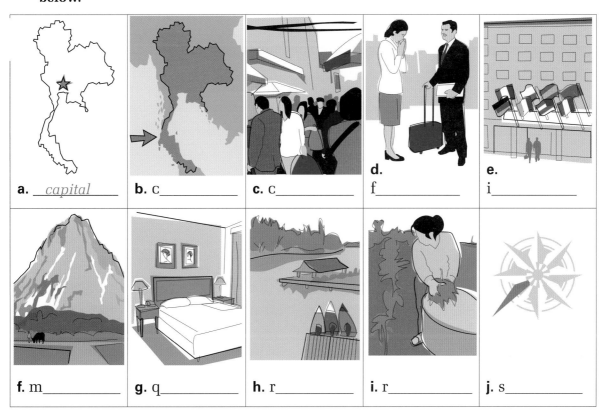

a. _capital_   **b.** c_____   **c.** c_____   **d.** f_____   **e.** i_____

f. m_____   **g.** q_____   **h.** r_____   **i.** r_____   **j.** s_____

a	h	y	i	v	c	r	o	w	d	e	d	t
m	o	u	n	t	a	i	n	b	b	k	a	e
b	u	k	a	k	e	q	w	n	g	h	k	r
x	d	s	f	b	m	m	c	v	q	t	e	u
t	c	o	a	s	t	s	f	h	v	w	h	r
j	j	u	e	z	x	c	j	h	t	k	x	a
i	n	t	e	r	n	a	t	i	o	n	a	l
q	e	h	t	u	u	p	o	t	d	f	j	v
d	r	w	t	q	u	i	e	t	x	z	q	m
g	k	e	s	t	a	t	g	b	z	x	n	v
q	x	s	v	a	n	a	j	r	i	v	e	r
l	p	t	h	e	o	l	x	r	e	c	t	m
f	r	i	e	n	d	l	y	d	l	u	o	m

3

Put it together: <u>I am from</u> poem

Where are you from? Of course, you are from a city and a country. But you are also "from" your family, your childhood, your activities, your memories, and your values—the ideas that are important to you.

a Complete this chart. Write two or three nouns in each space.

hobbies or interests:	things in your house:	things or places in your neighborhood:
names of friends and relatives:	food or dishes you ate when you were a child:	family vacations, trips, or holidays:
sports, activities, or games you play:	favorite school subjects or clubs:	favorite TV shows, movies, books, or music:
your hometown or places you have lived:	special family customs:	family values (example: *love, truth, home*):

b **Read this poem by a Thai student.**

I am from volleyball, bicycling, and tennis,
And I am from mango and sticky rice, and my mother's green curry.
I am from temples, markets, and the river,
And I am from shopping with my friends and eating noodles late at night.
I am from my king, my parents, and my teachers,
And I am from water festivals, flowers, and smiles.
I am from pop music CDs and traditional dance lessons,
And I am from beach vacations and working in the city.
I am from Bangkok, and I am from Thailand,
But most of all, I am from love.

c **Now use the ideas in the chart to write your poem. Begin every line with *I am from*. Use a separate sheet of paper.**

d   **Share your poem with a small group or the whole class.**

4 She seems lonely

In this unit, you will …
- learn vocabulary to describe people and their feelings
- learn a sentence pattern for stative verbs (*seems, looks*)
- learn a new sentence pattern for the be verb: *There is / There are*
- expand sentences with adverb phrases of location (*in the corner, at the back*)

I Work with a partner. Look at the people below. Complete the sentences using adjectives from the box.

cheerful	energetic	entertained	relaxed	✓shy

a. 1 She *is shy.* ....
2 *She is not* ....outgoing.

b. 1 They ....
2 .... lazy.

c. 1 He .... and ....
2 .... bored and depressed.

d. 1 He .... tense.
2 ....

2 Work with a partner. Look at the picture of the woman below. Talk about her and complete the chart.

Her job: ....   Her nationality: ....

Her age: ....   Her feelings now: ....

....

3 Now share your guesses with another pair, like this:

We think she's a student. What do you think?

4 Work with a partner. Read the sentences about the woman in exercise 2. Circle A if you agree the sentence is true. Circle D if you disagree.

a.	She seems lonely.	A	D
b.	She looks poor.	A	D
c.	I think she is unhappy.	A	D
d.	She seems healthy.	A	D
e.	She looks pretty.	A	D
f.	Maybe she is shy.	A	D

Stative verbs

Stative verbs:

- describe a condition or situation that exists
- do not show actions
- are followed by adjectives

  *She **seems** shy.* = stative ("shy" is a condition; it is also an adjective)

  *You **don't look** happy.*

noun or pronoun	stative verb	adjective
I You We They	seem don't seem	friendly. shy. happy.
He She	looks doesn't look	sad.

Some common stative verbs are *be, believe, have, know, like, think*.

Note: Stative verbs do not usually take the continuous tense:
RIGHT: *She seems happy.*
WRONG: *She is seeming happy.*

Sentence patterns with stative verbs

Look at these sentences from exercise 4 on page 30:

  *She **seems** lonely.*

  *She **looks** poor.*

The verbs *look* and *seem* show that the writer is not sure about the truth, but is just guessing.

Two sentences use the verb *be*. The writer shows that he or she is just guessing by beginning the sentences with *I think* and *Maybe*:

  ***I think** she is unhappy.*

  ***Maybe** she is shy.*

5 Write the sentences from exercise 4 again. Change the sentences with *look* and *seem* to use the verb *be*. Begin with *I think* or *Maybe*.

a. ....

b. ....

c. ....

d. ....

Now change the sentences with *be* to use *looks* or *seems*.

e. ....

f. ....

6 Look at the photo with a partner. Talk about what you see. Then complete the sentences with your own ideas. Read your sentences to another pair of students.

a. I think this man is a ....

b. He is .... and ....

c. He looks ....

d. Maybe he is ....

e. He seems ....

f. He doesn't look ....

There is / There are

	verb	noun	prepositional phrase of location
There	is	a little girl	on the bus.
	isn't	a secretary	in the office.
There	are	(some) girls	in the apartment.
	aren't	any men	in my class.

There + be shows that something exists: a thing (*a house, a cat, an elevator*) or an idea (*trouble, a thought*).

Usually we give more information by adding an adverb or prepositional phrase that shows a location:

There is a new student **in our class.**

There are some people **outside the building.**

There aren't any people **at the park.**

Prepositions of place

7 Work with a partner. Look at the picture of a classroom below. Then complete the paragraph on page 34 with the correct names.

Luis   Peter   Mrs. Hart   Jin-hee   Rico   Li

*This is my English class. There is a whiteboard **at the front of** the classroom. _____ is **in front of** the whiteboard. She always seems energetic and happy. There is a student **next to** the window **on the left**. His name is _____. He is not interested in English. He looks bored. There is a tall student **next to** Luis **on the right**. His name is _____. I think he is from Germany. There is a boy from Italy **next to** the wall **on the right**. He is **under** the clock. _____ likes English, but he seems tired today. There is a good student **between** Rico **and** Peter. Her name is _____. She's from Korea, and she's very friendly. I think Peter likes her. Where am I? I'm **behind** Rico. My name is _____. I'm from Malaysia. This is my favorite class.*

The prepositional phrase that shows location can also come at the beginning of the sentence:

*There is a new student **in our class**.*
***In our class**, there is a new student.*
*There are some people **outside the building**.*
***Outside the building**, there are some people.*

When the prepositional phrase begins the sentence, put a comma after it.

8   **Work with a partner. Write two sentences from each group of words. Remember to use a comma if necessary.**

a. there is / a whiteboard / of the classroom / at the front

There is a whiteboard at the front of the classroom.

At the front of the classroom, there is a whiteboard.

b. a bored student / on the left / there is / next to the wall

....

....

c. on the right / a tall student / next to Luis / there is

....

....

d. next to the wall / there is / on the right / a boy from Italy

....

....

9 **Circle the letter of the sentences that are correct.**

a. Near my apartment, there is a park.

b. There is some young children in the park today.

c. There is a little girl on the slide.

d. There are some noisy boy on the swings.

e. Under the tree, there are two birds.

f. On the bench, there are a young woman.

g. There aren't any man in the park.

h. By the gate, there is a police officer.

10 **Work with a partner. Look at the incorrect sentences in exercise 9 above. Write them again correctly on a separate sheet of paper.**

11 **Work with a partner. Look at the classroom. What's wrong? Talk about what you see.**

12 **Write sentences on a separate sheet of paper. Then compare your sentences with another pair.**

Spelling review

13 **Which word is spelled incorrectly? Circle the word. Then spell the word correctly.**

a. left   lonly   whiteboard   *lonely* ....

b. bord   lazy   shy   ....

c. frendly   happy   poor   ....

d. tense   outgoing   depresed   ....

e. behind   wright   between   ....

f. cheerful   relaxed   pritty   ....

g. outeside   front   next   ....

h. unhappy   energtic   healthy   ....

4

Put it together: Who is in apartment 6?

a Look at the people in the apartment building and choose one apartment. On a separate sheet of paper, write a description of the person or people inside. Write about what you can see, and also what you can guess. Do NOT write the apartment number.

> *In this apartment, there is a young man.*
>
> *I think he is a student. He is tall and thin.*
>
> *He seems tense. Maybe …*

b Work in small groups. Take turns reading your descriptions to the group. Can they

> I think it is the person in Apartment 5.

> Yes, that's correct! / Sorry, that's incorrect.

guess which person or people you wrote about?

c Who is in apartment 6? Complete the chart below from your imagination.

man or woman?	age:	nationality:
job:	description:	his/her feelings now:

d Write at least six sentences on a separate sheet of paper about the person in Apartment 6.

e Share your favorite words and sentences about the person in Apartment 6. Read your description to the whole class or a small group and listen to your classmates. Close your eyes. Can you "see" the person in Apartment 6 in your mind?

5 *She has brown eyes*

In this unit, you will …

- ■ learn vocabulary to describe animals and people
- ■ learn a sentence pattern for the *have* verb
- ■ learn when to use *a* and *an*
- ■ describe people with *be* and *have*

I   Work with a partner. Look at the pictures below. Label the parts of the animals.

beak	fin	mouth	tail
ear	fur	neck	tooth (plural: teeth)
feather	leg	nose	wing

a _ _ _ _ _ _

b _ _ _ _ _ _

The blue shark is from the Atlantic, Pacific, and Indian oceans.

c _ _ _ _ _ _

d _ _ _ _ _ _

This cute numbat is from Australia.

e _ _ _ _ _ _

f _ _ _ _ _ _

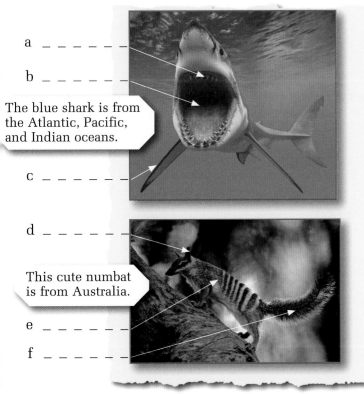

The Arabian gazelle is from the desert.

g _ _ _ _ _ _

h _ _ _ _ _ _

i _ _ _ _ _ _

j _ _ _ _ _ _

k _ _ _ _ _ _

l _ _ _ _ _ _

The quetzal is the national bird of Guatemala.

MEET ENDANGERED ANIMALS FROM AROUND THE WORLD

2   Work with a partner. Complete each sentence by writing *has* or *doesn't have*.

a. The quetzal .... colorful feathers.

b. The gazelle .... long legs.

c. The numbat .... wings.

d. The shark .... sharp teeth.

e. The numbat .... striped fur.

f. The quetzal .... large eyes.

g. The gazelle .... a long tail.

h. The shark .... a blue fin.

The *have* verb

noun or pronoun	verb	noun
I You We They	have don't have	long legs. short legs.
He She It	has doesn't have	a tail. wings.

Sentence patterns with *have*

Look at these sentences from exercise 2 on page 37:

The quetzal has colorful feathers.

The gazelle has long legs.

The numbat has striped fur.

The shark has a blue fin.

These sentences show something (*feathers, legs, fur, a fin*) that is part of the animal. The words after *have* are nouns.

It's possible to write:

The numbat has a tail.

The gazelle has legs.

However, we usually use an adjective before the noun:

*The numbat has a **beautiful** tail.*

*The gazelle has **long** legs.*

3 **Complete the sentences about the animals on page 37 by writing an adjective. Then share your sentences with a partner.**

a. The quetzal doesn't have .... legs.

b. The numbat has .... ears.

c. The shark has .... teeth.

d. The gazelle has a(n) .... neck.

e. The shark doesn't have a(n) .... tail.

f. The quetzal has a(n) .... beak.

g. The gazelle doesn't have .... fur.

Using a and an

- Remember to use *a* or *an* in front of a singular noun—even if there is an adjective in front of it.

  *The gazelle has **a nose.***

  *It has **a long nose.***

- Don't use *a* or *an* in front of plural words (look for the ~s ending!).

  *The quetzal has **wings.***

  *It has black **eyes.***

- Some words in English can't be singular or plural. Don't use *a* or *an* in front of these words:

  *The cat has nice **fur.***

  *A shark doesn't have **hair.***

4 **Read the sentences below and correct the mistake in each one.**

  a. The shark doesn't have a hair.

  b. The quetzal has soft wing.

  c. The gazelle has strong neck.

  d. The numbat has a brown ears.

  e. The shark has a many teeth.

  f. The quetzal doesn't have a fur.

  g. The numbat has cute nose.

5 **Look at the photos below. With a partner, write sentences with your own ideas on a separate sheet of paper. Then read your sentences to another pair. Were any of your sentences the same?**

ostrich

wolf

6 Think of an animal. Write at least five sentences about it. Then read your sentences to a partner. Can your partner guess the animal?

....

....

....

....

....

> It has four legs and a short tail. It has a long gray nose.

> Is it an elephant?

Vocabulary for describing people

7 Look at the picture on the right. Then complete the paragraph about people with *have* or *don't have*.

People are animals, but they are different too. For example, people don't have fur. They _____ hair. They _____ skin, not feathers. People _____ wings or fins. They _____ arms and legs. People _____ hands, too, with fingers. People and animals _____ eyes, ears, a nose, and a mouth.

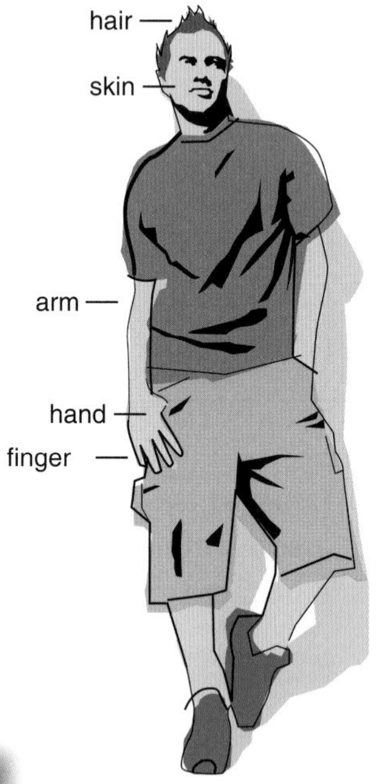

hair —
skin —
arm —
hand —
finger —

8 Complete the paragraph with *a*, *an*, or ∅ (nothing).

I have _____ new sister! She's very pretty. She has _____ small body and _____ big head. She has _____ big brown eyes, but she doesn't have _____ much hair. She has _____ tiny hands and _____ cute little fingers. She has _____ soft skin and _____ nice smile. I love my baby sister.

Have and *be*

In Units 3 and 4, you described people using *be*. In this unit, you described people using *have*:

My father **is** an engineer.   She **has** big brown eyes.

He **is** tall.   My baby sister **has** soft skin.

I think he **is** friendly.   She **has** a nice smile.

> **Remember:** Use **be** with a noun that:
> • means the same thing as the subject:
> She **is** a baby.
> • describes the subject:
> She **is** cute.
> • tells where the subject is:
> She **is** in the living room.
> Use **have** with parts of the body that belong to the subject:
> She **has** large eyes.

9 Look at the photo album. Complete the descriptions by writing the correct form of *be* or *have*.

Friends at my school

This is Maya. She _____ in my math class. In this picture, she _____ long hair, but now she _____ short hair. I think the short hair _____ cute. She seems shy, but she _____ friendly. She _____ very smart, and she _____ a good friend.

This _____ Ian. He _____ an exchange student from New Zealand. He _____ big hands, and he
_____ long fingers. He _____ a very good guitar player. He _____ short brown hair and a kind face. He _____ tall and thin.

Who _____ pretty hair? Greta! I think she _____ beautiful. She _____ long red hair and green eyes. She _____ nice skin, a small nose, and small ears. She _____ tall, too. But she _____ not very nice. I don't know why.

10 A UFO landed last night! What do the aliens look like?

a Work with a partner. What words can you use to describe the aliens?

b Write sentences about them. Check to see that you used *have* and *be* correctly.

....

....

....

....

c Share your sentences with another pair. Did you write any similar sentences?

Spelling review

11 One <u>underlined</u> word in each sentence is spelled incorrectly. Circle it, and then write the correct spelling above.

a. The model has a small *nose* (noze) and <u>beautiful</u> hair.

b. My cat has <u>soft</u> gray <u>furr</u>.

c. The condor has black <u>feithers</u> and a long <u>beak</u>.

d. My <u>friend</u> is short, and she has <u>tiney</u> feet.

e. That man <u>dosen't</u> have any <u>hair</u>.

f. The baby has small <u>handes</u> and nice <u>skin</u>.

g. The numbat is <u>stripied</u>, and it has sharp <u>teeth</u>.

Put it together: A photo album

Imagine you are making a photo album. You can use real photos, draw pictures, or just write descriptions.

a   Choose a theme for your album. For example, *My Classmates, My Family, My Friends, Interesting Animals, Celebrities, Alien Visitors.*

Write it here: _____

b   Write descriptions of at least four people or animals. First write your ideas in the word web below. Use the correct forms of *have* and *be* in your notes. Use *a* or *an* if necessary.

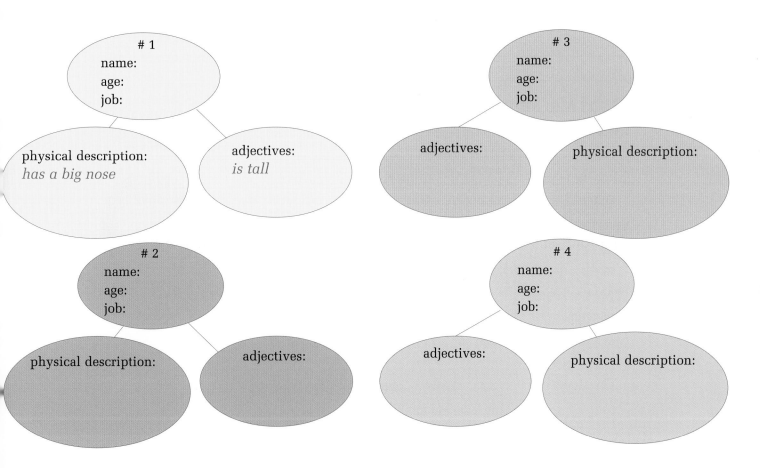

1
name:
age:
job:

physical description:
has a big nose

adjectives:
is tall

2
name:
age:
job:

physical description:

adjectives:

3
name:
age:
job:

adjectives:

physical description:

4
name:
age:
job:

adjectives:

physical description:

Now write descriptions of each person or animal. Use a separate sheet of paper.

d   ⬚ Share your ideas with a small group. Take turns reading your descriptions. If you have pictures, show them to your group. Make one comment about each description you hear.

He sounds scary!

Your mother sounds nice.

6 *I like playing soccer*

In this unit, you will …

■ learn vocabulary to talk about hobbies and interests

■ learn a sentence pattern for action verbs

■ learn to combine words with *and*, *but*, and *or*

■ learn to use gerunds

I Work with a partner. Look at the website below. Write the verbs from the box in the correct place.

| go | have | like (x 2) | live | read | speak | watch |

About Me: **Sung-woo.**

Nationality/hometown: I'm Korean. I _____ in Pusan. Pusan is a large city on the coast.

School or work: I _____ to Pusan University of Foreign Studies. I'm a first-year student. I'm studying English and Japanese.

Favorites:

Activities: I _____ playing and watching soccer. Playing soccer is good exercise.

TV Shows: I don't _____ TV. I watch DVDs and movies sometimes.

Movies: I like science fiction and action movies. I don't like sad or scary movies.

Books: I don't _____ books or magazines. I like anime. I _____ many Japanese comic books!

Music: I like listening to rock and pop music. My favorite singer is BoA. Her full name is BoA Kwon. She's Korean. She is popular in Japan too. She speaks Japanese very well!

Food: My favorite food is kimchi. My favorite dessert is ice cream. I also _____ making sushi.

Friends: My best friend's name is Hiro. He's Japanese. I play soccer with him. I _____ Japanese with him too.

Photos

Sung-woo

2 **Work with a partner. Complete the sentences with information from page 44.**

a. Sung-woo lives in ....*Pusan*.. .

b. He's studying ....

c. He likes playing .... and .... soccer.

d. He doesn't like ....

e. He likes reading ....

f. BoA speaks .... very well.

Action verbs with objects

Action verbs show what the subject is doing.

Subject	verb	noun (direct object)	prepositional phrase
I You We They	play	the piano	on Saturday.
He She	is reading	a book	in the library.

Sentence patterns with action verbs

It's possible in English to write a sentence with just a subject and an action verb:

He reads.

I play.

Usually, though, something comes after the action verb, such as

- a phrase that shows a place:

    *He reads **on the train**.*

- a phrase that shows a time:

    *He reads **on the weekends**.*

- a noun that receives the action of the verb, called a *direct object*:

    *I play **soccer**.*

- a combination of a direct object and a phrase that shows a place or time (or both):

    *I play **soccer in the park**.*

    *I play **soccer after school**.*

    *I play **soccer in the park after school**.*

3 Work with a partner. Add the words and phrases to the chart. Then add two of your own ideas to each column.

✓ at college	in the supermarket	French	teach
practice	tennis	at 6:30	in the morning
study	✓ the men	my friends and I	the guitar
you	my teacher	sing	✓ play
in the kitchen	on Sunday	✓ chess	songs

subject	verb	direct object (noun)	prepositional phrase of time or place
The men	play	chess	at college.

4 Make sentences from the chart above. Make sure your subjects and verbs agree! Then compare your sentences with a partner.

a. ....

b. ....

c. ....

d. ....

e. ....

f. ....

g. ....

h. ....

Combining words with <u>and</u> and <u>or</u>

Combining words in one sentence makes your sentences sound more fluent. Here are two ways to do this:

- Use *and* to combine two words that are similar:

    I like cake. I like ice cream.
    *I like cake **and** ice cream.*

- Use *or* to combine two similar words after a negative verb:

    I don't play baseball. I don't play basketball.
    *I don't play baseball **or** soccer.*

> **Note:** Combine the same kind of words (for example, two nouns or two adjectives).

5 **Write the correct form of the verb.**

  a. Kendra ...*plays*........................ basketball and tennis. (play)

  b. I .... cats or dogs. (like)

  c. My teacher .... French and Arabic. (know)

  d. My sister .... the piano and the violin. (play)

  e. We .... in a small or quiet town. (live)

  f. My best friend .... Chinese or Thai. (speak)

Combining words with <u>but</u>

- Use *but* to combine two words that don't usually go together. *But* shows that the information is surprising. *But* is often used in this way with adjectives:

    She is small. She is strong.
    *She is small **but** strong.*

6 **Complete the sentences by circling the best word.**

  a. This book is long but *tall / interesting.*

  b. Our teacher was surprised but *happy / angry.*

  c. My phone was cheap but *good / new.*

  d. I feel happy but *sad / tired.*

  e. Today is sunny but *cold / warm.*

  f. The pizza was simple but *delicious / cheap.*

7 Complete the following sentences with *and*, *or*, or *but*.

a. I'm not a high school student .... a university student.

b. I'm an office worker .... an artist.

c. During the week, I work in an office in the center of the city.
My work is hard .... interesting.

d. I'm an artist on Saturday .... Sunday.

e. I don't paint .... draw.

f. I take photographs of people .... animals.

g. I give my photos to friends .... family.

h. I'm very busy .... happy.

8 Write true sentences about yourself with *and*, *or*, and *but*. Then share your sentences with a partner.

a. (and) ....

b. (but) ....

c. (or) ....

Gerunds

Gerunds are nouns made from verbs. They end with ~*ing*.

Look at these examples. Notice how the gerunds are in the same position in the sentence as a regular noun:

I like sports.
I like baseball and tennis.
*I like **playing** soccer.*
*I like **swimming** and **skiing**.*

Gerunds are common after these verbs: *like, enjoy, can't stand, hate*.

Because they are nouns, gerunds can also be sentence subjects:

***Playing** baseball is fun.*
***Swimming** is good exercise.*
***Making** movies is an interesting hobby.*

Note: Don't confuse a gerund with the present continuous.

A gerund is a noun:

I like ***swimming***. (*swimming* is a noun. You could also say, I like ***sports***.)

The present continuous is a verb tense. It is made with the be verb:

I am ***swimming***. (*swimming* is a verb. You could also say, I am ***walking***.)

Spelling and gerunds

Look at these rules for spelling gerunds:

v = vowel (a, e, i, o, u)

c = consonant (b, c, d, f, g, h, j, k, l, m, n, p, q, r, s, t, v, w, x, y, z)

If the word ends with

- c + c (wa**lk**, thi**nk**)

then add ~*ing* (walk**ing**, think**ing**)

- v + v + c (sp**eak**, r**ead**)

then add ~*ing* (speak**ing**, read**ing**)

- c + v + c, and the word is one syllable (**run**, s**top**)

then double the last consonant and add (~*ing*) (run**ning**, stop**ping**)

- v + c + the letter e (m**ake**, wr**ite**)

then drop the e and add ~*ing* (mak**ing**, writ**ing**)

> **Remember:** These rules are *usually* true. They are not *always* true.

9 **Write the gerund form of the following words.**

- **a.** live ....
- **b.** eat ....
- **c.** shop ....
- **d.** sing ....
- **e.** study ....

- **f.** cook ....
- **g.** drive ....
- **h.** swim ....
- **i.** take ....
- **j.** watch ....

10 **Look back at the website on page 44. Copy the four sentences with gerunds.**

- **a.** ....
- **b.** ....
- **c.** ....
- **d.** ....

One sentence uses the present continuous. Write it here:

- **e.** ....

11 Complete these sentences that begin with gerunds. You can use an adjective or a noun. Then share your sentences with a partner.

a. Cooking is ....

b. Reading novels is ....

c. Swimming is ....

d. Studying English is ....

e. Listening to music is ....

f. Exercising is ....

12 Complete the following sentences with gerunds. Then share your sentences with a classmate.

a. I can't stand ....

b. My favorite sport is ....

c. On weekends I hate ....

d. On rainy days I like ....

e. I enjoy ....

f. My parents don't like ....

g. .... is boring.

h. .... is my friend's hobby.

i. .... is fun.

j. .... is difficult.

Spelling review

13 Write the missing letters.

a. bas ___ b ___ ll

b. exer ___ ___ ___ e

c. fav ___ ___ ___ te

d. int ___ ___ ___ sting

e. Kor ___ ___ n

f. lis ___ ___ ning

g. p ___ pul ___ r

h. delic ___ ___ ___ s

i. stud ___ ___ ng

j. wri ___ ___ ___ g

Put it together: Your personal website

You are going to make a personal website. You can make more than one page if you want.

a What do you want to write about? Make notes in the chart below. You can also use your own ideas.

About you (name, home, school)	activities & interests	likes / dislikes
family:	friends:	favorite music / food:

b On a separate sheet of paper, design your website and write your information. Start like this:

Hello! Welcome to _____'s website. Here you can learn a little about me. I hope you enjoy this site.

Try to use *and*, *or*, *but*, and gerunds.

c Share your web page. Move around the classroom speaking to one person at a time. If your classmate has a similar interest or hobby, "link" to his or her web page by writing his or her name and underlining it. See how many classmates you can link to!

7 Faded jeans are cool

In this unit, you will …

■ learn vocabulary for describing clothing and fashion

■ write sentences with subject and object pronouns

■ combine sentences with *and*, *but*, *or*, and *so*

■ put two or three adjectives in the correct order

I Work with a partner. Read the fashion blog. Write the <u>underlined</u> expressions next to the correct pictures.

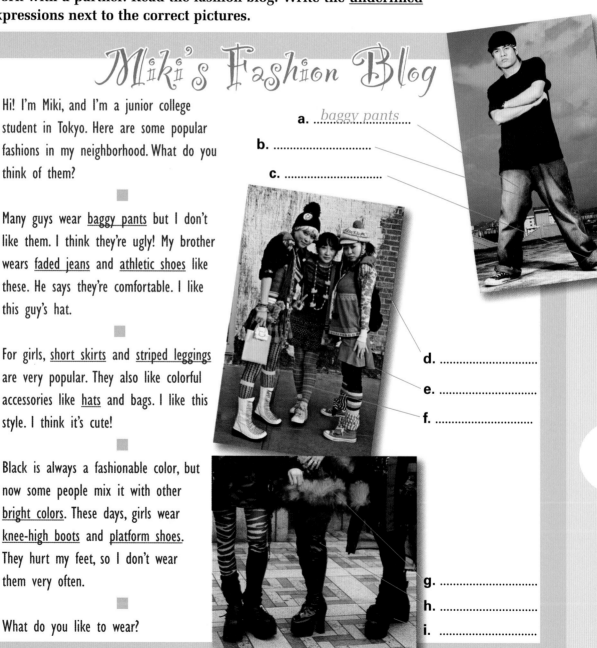

Miki's Fashion Blog

Hi! I'm Miki, and I'm a junior college student in Tokyo. Here are some popular fashions in my neighborhood. What do you think of them?

Many guys wear <u>baggy pants</u> but I don't like them. I think they're ugly! My brother wears <u>faded jeans</u> and <u>athletic shoes</u> like these. He says they're comfortable. I like this guy's hat.

For girls, <u>short skirts</u> and <u>striped leggings</u> are very popular. They also like colorful accessories like <u>hats</u> and bags. I like this style. I think it's cute!

Black is always a fashionable color, but now some people mix it with other <u>bright colors</u>. These days, girls wear <u>knee-high boots</u> and <u>platform shoes</u>. They hurt my feet, so I don't wear them very often.

What do you like to wear?

a. *baggy pants* ....

b. ....

c. ....

d. ....

e. ....

f. ....

g. ....

h. ....

i. ....

2 Do you like these fashions? Write true sentences with *I like* or *I don't like*.
Then share your sentences with a partner.

a. .... striped pants. **d**. .... faded clothing.

b. .... baggy jeans. **e**. .... platform boots.

c. .... athletic pants. **f**. .... black leggings.

3 Work with a partner. Are these adjectives positive or negative?
Write them in the correct column.

| ✓ comfortable | silly | cool | ugly |
| cute | unattractive | fashionable | uncomfortable |

positive	negative
....	....
....	....
....	....
....	....

4 Write one adjective from exercise 3 (or use your own ideas, such as a color) for
each piece of clothing.

.... cap
.... scarf
.... T-shirt
.... belt
.... bag
.... shorts
.... socks

5 Work with a partner. What other types of clothing are the people in your class
wearing today? Make a list. Use a dictionary if necessary.

....
....
....
....

Subject and object pronouns

subject		*be* verb	adjective
My scarf It	}	is	old.
Platform shoes They	}	are	uncomfortable.

subject	verb	object	
My brother	likes	{	his faded T-shirt. it.
I	want	{	knee-high boots. them.

- Use *it* for singular nouns (both subjects and objects).
- Use *they* for plural subject nouns.
- Use *them* for plural object nouns.

6 **Draw a line to connect the sentences that go together. Use the pronouns as clues.**

a. My blue jeans are very old.		**1.** They are black.	
b. I like that scarf.		**2.** I keep my cell phone in it.	
c. I like my new boots.		**3.** I can't wear them.	
d. I don't like that short skirt.		**4.** I wear them with my athletic shoes.	
e. I have new white socks.		**5.** It's not fashionable.	
f. This bag is cute.		**6.** It's very long.	

7 **Write about the clothing below. Use:**

- I wear / I don't wear
- subject and object pronouns
- an adverb of frequency
- adjectives

a. leggings   *I never wear them. They're silly.*

b. my jacket   *I often wear it. It's comfortable.*

c. platform shoes   ....

d. baggy pants   ....

e. my outfit today   ....

f. my favorite T-shirt   ....

g. brand-name jeans   ....

h. my watch   ....

Combining sentences with <u>and</u>, <u>but</u>, <u>or</u>, and <u>so</u>

Use *and*, *but*, *or*, and *so* to join two complete sentences.

- *and* shows similar activities or feelings:

    *I like my hat, **and** I often wear it.*

    *I like bright yellow, **and** I like bright pink.*

- *but* shows a contrast or difference:

    *I wear a uniform to school, **but** I wear fashionable clothing at home.*

    *I have some pink socks, **but** I never wear them.*

- *or* shows two choices or alternatives:

    *You can buy the boots, **or** you can buy the shoes.*

    *On weekends, I wear baggy pants, **or** I wear my faded jeans.*

- *so* shows that the second sentence is a result of the first one:

    *Brand-name clothing is expensive, **so** I rarely buy it.*

    *I don't like my hat, **so** I never wear it.*

Note: Use a comma before ***and***, ***but***, ***or***, and ***so*** when you combine two complete sentences.

8 Look back at the blog on page 52. Write the sentences that show two complete sentences combined with these words:

a. (and) ....

b. (but) ....

c. (but) ....

d. (and) ....

e. (so) ....

9 Work with a partner. Combine the two sentences with *and*, *but*, *or*, or *so*. Write a comma in the correct place.

    a. I like long skirts. I often wear them.

    ....

    b. My jeans are very faded. I want new jeans.

    ....

    c. I'm very busy. I'm not going shopping.

    ....

    d. I can wear my old jacket. I can buy a new one.

    ....

    e. I have a lot of fashionable clothes. I never wear them.

    ....

10 Complete the sentences. Then share your sentences with a partner.

    a. I don't like this shirt, so ....

    b. I wear a uniform to school, but ....

    c. I'm wearing socks today, and ....

    d. You can buy the pink leggings, or ....

    e. I like baggy pants, but ....

    f. This dress is uncomfortable, so ....

Combining adjectives

Often English writers use two adjectives to describe a noun, and sometimes even three adjectives. The chart shows which adjectives come first.

opinion	size	age	color	material	noun
	large		white		shirt
		new		leather	watch
strange	little				hat
ugly		old	black		jacket
			pink	cotton	dress

11 **Work with a partner. Write the words in the box into the chart above. Can you add any other words?**

big	cute	pretty	silk	sweater	wool
brown	mini	purple	small	unusual	yellow

Note: We usually say *little old* and not *small old*.

12 Complete the sentences with an adjective from the chart or your own idea.

a. I don't like .... leather shoes.

b. I'm wearing a large .... cotton shirt.

c. That's an ugly .... dress.

d. Do you have a long .... scarf?

e. I have a / an .... black jacket.

f. She likes .... purple boots.

13 Write at least five true sentences about what you are wearing today. Then share your sentences with a partner. Use a separate sheet of paper.

Spelling review

14 **Complete the crossword puzzle.**

across

5. Many people think colorful accessories are c... .

6. These boots are very small. They're u... .

7. I play sports in my a... shoes.

8. I like b... colors like pink and yellow.

10. She usually wears l... with her skirt.

12. Do you like p... shoes?

down

1. I don't often wear brand-name c... .

3. I wear a wool s... in the winter.

4. This is a l... belt.

6. Don't buy that jacket. It's u... now.

9. Baggy pants are s... . I don't like them.

11. My favorite color is p... .

Put it together: A fashion blog

a What do people in your neighborhood or school wear? Write notes.

clothing	like or don't like?	opinion
faded jeans	*like*	*they're cool*

b Choose three or more fashions. Write blog entries. Follow the examples on page 52. If you like, you can draw pictures or cut out photographs of the fashions.

c  Share your work in small groups. Read your blog entries to your group. Do they have the same opinions or different opinions? Are there any fashions that everyone likes? Are there any fashions that everyone dislikes?

> I agree! I think faded clothing is fashionable.

> I don't agree. I think faded clothing is ugly.

8 I'm a business major

In this unit, you will …

- learn vocabulary for school subjects
- use the simple present and present progressive tenses
- learn adverbs and expressions of frequency
- learn the format of a paragraph

I Work with a partner. Read about the students. Then use the <u>underlined</u> words to label the pictures on page 61. Can you do it without a dictionary?

I'm a <u>business</u> major. I like my business classes. I'm also taking a <u>math</u> class, but I'm not getting good grades now. I rarely study. I don't like numbers very much.

Samira

I'm studying <u>art</u>. I love drawing and painting. I usually paint in my studio, but sometimes I paint outside. I like playing the piano too, so next term I'm taking a <u>music</u> class.

Paulo

I'm good at <u>foreign languages</u>. My favorite subject is English, and I'm also studying Spanish and French. I'm an <u>international studies</u> major.

Jee-hyun

I'm in high school, so I don't have a major. My father is a doctor, and I think that's interesting. I also enjoy playing baseball all the time, so I'm thinking about studying <u>sports medicine</u>.

Takeshi

I play video games all the time—every morning, every evening, and every weekend! I enjoy designing video games too. I'm a <u>computer science</u> major, of course!

Tyler

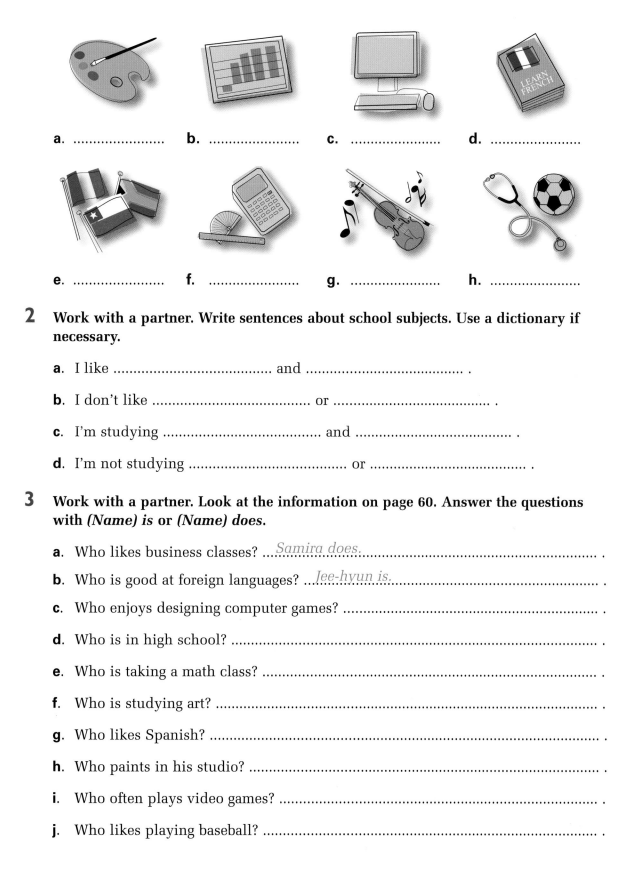

a. .... b. .... c. .... d. ....

e. .... f. .... g. .... h. ....

2 Work with a partner. Write sentences about school subjects. Use a dictionary if necessary.

a. I like .... and ....

b. I don't like .... or ....

c. I'm studying .... and ....

d. I'm not studying .... or ....

3 Work with a partner. Look at the information on page 60. Answer the questions with *(Name) is* or *(Name) does*.

a. Who likes business classes? ...*Samira does.*...

b. Who is good at foreign languages? ...*Jee-hyun is.*..................................

c. Who enjoys designing computer games? ....

d. Who is in high school? ....

e. Who is taking a math class? ....

f. Who is studying art? ....

g. Who likes Spanish? ....

h. Who paints in his studio? ....

i. Who often plays video games? ....

j. Who likes playing baseball? ....

Verb tense: The simple present

Use the simple present

- for actions that you do regularly:
  I **play** the piano.
  I **drive** to work.

- to describe something that's always true about you:
  I **like** chocolate.
  I**'m** a French major.

- with expressions like *always, usually, sometimes, never*:
  I <u>often</u> **sleep** late.
  I <u>never</u> **watch** TV.

- with expressions like *on Saturdays, every week, in the afternoon*:
  I **play** soccer <u>every weekend</u>.
  I **have** a math class <u>on Tuesdays</u>.

> **Note:** Remember to use *do / does* to make questions and negative statements with action verbs.
>
> *Do you play the piano?*   *No, I don't.*
> *Does she like chocolate?*   *No, she doesn't.*

4 **Complete the questions with *Do*, *Does*, *Are*, or *Is*. Then match them to the answers.**

a. *Do* .... you have a major?

b. .... your friend like foreign languages?

c. .... you good at math?

d. .... you usually get good grades?

e. .... your business class in the morning?

f. .... your sister play sports?

g. .... you like playing music?

h. .... your friend in college?

1. Yes, he does. He's a Chinese major.

2. Yes, I am. I love math!

3. Yes, I do. I'm a science major.

4. No, she doesn't. She doesn't like exercising.

5. No, I don't. I'm not good at music.

6. Yes, she is. She's a computer science major.

7. Yes, I do. I study hard!

8. No, it isn't. It's in the afternoon.

5 **Work with a partner. Write three questions for your partner. Then ask the questions and write a short answer. Then write a complete sentence about your partner.**

a. Do *you like English?*   *Yes, he does.*   *Hassan likes English.*

b. Do .... ?   ....

c. Does .... ?   ....

d. Are .... ?   ....

Adverbs of frequency

Look at the chart of adverbs and examples of expressions we use to write about how often something happens.

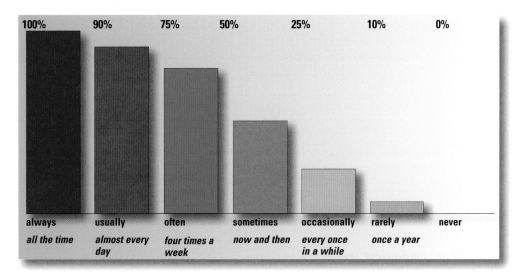

100%	90%	75%	50%	25%	10%	0%
always	usually	often	sometimes	occasionally	rarely	never
all the time	almost every day	four times a week	now and then	every once in a while	once a year	

- **Adverbs of frequency** go between the subject and an action verb:

    I **always** do my work.
    I **occasionally** ride by bike to school.

- However, they come after the *be* verb:

    I am **sometimes** lonely.
    I am **never** late.

- *Usually, often, sometimes,* and *occasionally* can also go before the subject:

    Usually I study with a friend.
    Sometimes I play games online.

- **Expressions of frequency** go after the verb at the end of the sentence, or before the subject at the beginning of the sentence. However, they are most common at the end of the sentence:

    I go to the movies **now and then.**
    Once a year, I take a vacation.

6 **Look back at the student profiles on page 60. Copy the sentences …**

- that have an adverb of frequency after the subject:

a. ....

b. ....

- that have an adverb of frequency before the subject:

c. ....

- that have an expression of frequency after the verb:

d. ....

7 Complete the following sentences with true information about yourself. Then compare your sentences with a partner.

a. I usually ....

b. I am rarely ....

c. I .... every once in a while.

d. I never ....

e. I .... almost every week.

f. I .... once or twice a year.

g. Usually I .... , but sometimes I ....

h. Often I ....

Verb tense: The present progressive

Use the present progressive

- for an action that's happening right now:
    I'm typing my paper.
    I'm having lunch.

- to describe a temporary action; something that you're doing now, and will continue in the future, but will end:
    I'm taking a dance class.
    I'm studying science.

- to talk about something you plan to do soon:
    I'm having dinner in a restaurant tonight.
    I'm traveling to Europe this summer.

> **Note:** Remember that the present progressive is almost never used with stative verbs, such as **be**, **have**, **think**, **feel**, **know**, etc. (see Unit 4, page 31).

8 Complete the sentences from page 60 with the correct form of the verb. Don't look until you're finished. Then check your answers.

a. Samira (not / get) .... good grades now.

b. Sometimes Paulo (paint) .... outside.

c. Jee-hyun (take) .... Spanish and French.

d. Takeshi (be) .... in high school.

e. Tyler (play) .... computer games all the time.

9 Answer the questions with true information about yourself. Write a short answer and a complete sentence. Then compare your sentences with a partner.

a. Do you have a major? *Yes, I do. I'm a business major.*
No, I don't. But I like computer science.

b. Are you a business major? ....

....

c. Are you taking music lessons? ....

....

d. Do you often play baseball? ....

....

e. Do you like math? ....

....

f. Are you usually good at foreign languages? ....

....

g. Are you studying science? ....

....

Paragraph format

In English writing, sentences are often arranged in paragraphs. Paragraphs have a special shape. Each paragraph is about one topic or idea. Every sentence in the paragraph gives some information about that topic. When you want to write about another topic, begin a new paragraph.

10 Work with a partner. Look at the examples below. Check (✓) the one that has the right shape for a paragraph in English. How can you describe that shape?

WHAT'S YOUR ZODIAC SIGN?

March 21 – April 19
You're an Aries.
You're active and outgoing.
You like being the leader and you like organizing things.
You always have a lot of ideas, and you like telling people what to do.
You're good at sports.
Sometimes you are too pushy! ☐

April 20 – May 20
You're a Taurus. You're calm and patient. Usually you like being alone, but you're lonely every once in a while. Sometimes other people don't understand you very well. You like animals and nature. Maybe you have a pet. ☐

May 21 – June 20
You're a Gemini.
You love people, and you talk all the time. You're usually good at making money, and you're always good at spending it.
Maybe you're an economics or a business major. A Gemini loves adventure and travel. ☐

11 Unscramble the sentences. Then copy them in correct paragraph format in the box below.

a / Cancer / you're

romantic / you're / interesting and

a lot of / you / friends / have

feel / you / every day / different almost

you / understand / your friends don't / always /

quiet and / sometimes you're / shy

June 21 – July 20

Spelling review

12 Write the missing letters to form common expressions.

a. business m ___ ___ ___ r

b. art s ___ ___ ___ ___ o

c. c ___ ___ ___ ___ ___ ___ r science

d. foreign l ___ ___ ___ ___ ___ ___ ___ s

e. high s ___ ___ ___ ___ l

f. international s ___ ___ ___ ___ ___ s

g. sports m ___ ___ ___ ___ ___ ___ e

h. v ___ ___ ___ o games

Put it together: A new zodiac

a   Create a new zodiac! Use the animals below or your own ideas.

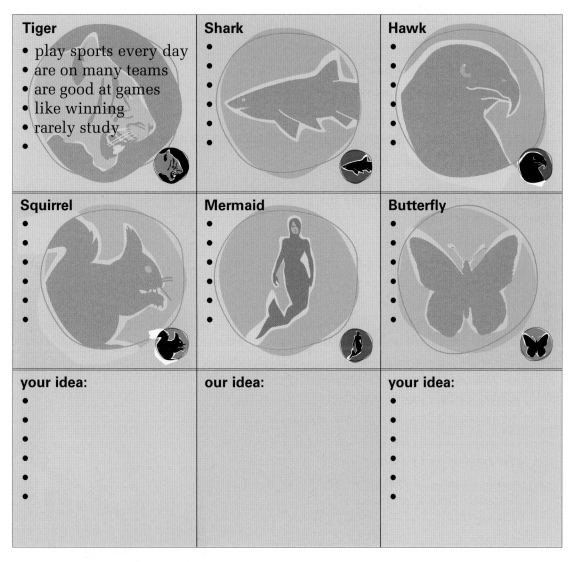

Tiger
- play sports every day
- are on many teams
- are good at games
- like winning
- rarely study
-

Shark
-
-
-
-
-

Hawk
-
-
-
-
-

Squirrel
-
-
-
-
-

Mermaid
-
-
-
-
-

Butterfly
-
-
-
-
-

your idea:
-
-
-
-
-
-

our idea:
-
-
-
-
-
-

your idea:
-
-
-
-
-
-

b   Choose three "new zodiac" signs. On a separate sheet of paper, write a short paragraph about each one. Use good paragraph format! Follow the example.

> *Tiger: You're an athlete. You play sports every day. You play baseball every spring and basketball every fall. You're also on the tennis team. You're good at games, and you like winning. You don't like school, and you rarely study.*

c   Share your new zodiac with a small group. Read your three paragraphs to the group. Can they think of any students who match your descriptions?

I think Jill is a Tiger.

9 I'm in Barcelona

In this unit, you will …

■ learn some irregular past tense verbs

■ learn to write sentences with indirect objects

■ learn how to format a postcard and an email

■ learn the difference between formal and informal language

■ use questions and exclamations

1 Work with a partner. Complete the postcard below with verbs from the box. One verb is not used.

ate	bought	got	had	sent	took	was	went

Dear Rachel,

   Hi! How are you? I'm having a great time. I'm in Barcelona now. We _____ here on Tuesday. Barcelona is beautiful! It's on the coast, so we went to the beach on Wednesday. It was hot and sunny. In the afternoon, we _____ to an art museum. Do you like the building on this card? It's a church. I _____ many photographs of it. Yesterday I went shopping. I _____ a T-shirt for my brother. Then we _____ lunch and _____ coffee in a café, and I _____ my family some postcards.
Your friend,
Liza

2 Next, Liza sent an email from an Internet café. Use the notes below to write complete sentences in the past tense. Write the sentences in correct paragraph form on page 69.

Guess what? I (meet) a Spanish man.

He (be) very handsome and friendly.

He (give) me a tour of Barcelona.

I (have) a good time.

He also (give) me his phone number and email address.

I (not call) him, but I (email) him my home address in Canada.

Hi Rachel,

....

....

....

....

....

See you soon,
Liza

Indirect objects

Noun	verb	noun (direct object)	preposition + noun (indirect object)
I	wrote	a letter	to Charlie.
You	gave	some money	to me.

Noun	verb	noun (indirect object)	noun (direct object)
I	wrote	Charlie	a letter.
You	gave	me	some money.

You know that direct objects receive the action of the verb (see page 45):

> I wrote **a letter.**
> You gave **some money.**

- *Indirect objects* receive the direct object. They can come after the direct object, with a preposition such as *to* or *for*:

> I wrote a letter **to Charlie.**
> You gave some money **to me.**

- Or they can come before the direct object, without a preposition:

> I wrote **Charlie** a letter.
> You gave **me** some money.

3 **Look back at the postcard on page 68. Copy the sentences with indirect objects …**

- that come after the direct object:

....

- that come before the direct object:

....

....

4 **Unscramble the sentences. Then write them again and move the indirect object.**

a. me / wrote / a poem / Carlos *Carlos wrote me a poem.*..

Carlos wrote a poem for me....

b. made / for / a scarf / I / my sister *I made a scarf for my sister.*......................................

I made my sister a scarf....

c. us / Min-hee / a letter/ sent ....

....

d. I / a cake / you / for / baked ....

....

e. to / our teacher / any homework / didn't give / us ....

....

f. emailed / her / a photo / Rashad ....

....

5 **Answer the questions. Use an indirect object in your answer.**

a. Did you send an email to someone? *Yes, I sent my parents an email.*..........................

b. Did you cook dinner for someone? ....

c. Did you buy someone a gift? ....

d. Did you do someone a favor? ....

e. Did you write a letter to someone? ....

f. Did you give someone a message? ....

Format of a postcard or email

Look at the postcard on page 68. Who wrote the postcard? Who will read it? How do you know?

Begin an email or postcard with the name of the person you are writing to:

Dear Rachel, / *Hi Rachel,*

End it with your name:

Your friend, / *See you soon,*
Liza *Liza*

The first line of an email or postcard is usually a greeting. What greeting did Liza use in her postcard?

Informal and formal language

When you write to someone you know well, like a friend or a family member, you use **informal language**. Use **very informal language** only with a close friend of about your same age.
When you write to someone you don't know well, or someone older or more important than you, you use **formal language**.

6 **Write the words and expressions into the correct place in the chart.**

Greetings	Questions	Closings
Hello.	Whassup?	Sincerely,
Yo!	How are you?	Catch ya later!
Hi.	How are you doing?	Your friend,

formal	informal	very informal
....	....	....
....	....	....
....	....	....

7 **Work with a partner or group. Discuss these questions.**
- What other informal or very informal words or writing styles do you know?
- In your own language, do you usually write with formal or informal language?
- List some people you know that you would use these styles with:

formal: ....

informal: ....

very informal: ....

8 Look at this email from Mike Smith, a student, to his professor, Dr. Brown. It is too informal. Write it again, in correct format, with more formal language. Then compare your email with a partner.

> Yo, Brownie! Whassup? I hope U R fine. Sorry I wuz late 2 class. ☹ Didja give NE homework 2 us? I hope not! Ha ha! I will C U in class 2morrow. Catch ya l8r.
>
> ....
>
> ....
>
> ....
>
> ....

Using questions and exclamations

Most sentences in English end with a period $\boxed{.}$. However, sentences can also end with a question mark $\boxed{?}$ or an exclamation mark $\boxed{!}$.

You know that a question mark is used with a question. When do you use an exclamation mark? Is it formal or informal? Look at the postcard and email on page 68 and find the sentences that end with a question mark or an exclamation mark.

> **Note:** Don't use too many exclamations in one paragraph. In formal writing, don't use more than one question mark or exclamation point at the end of one sentence.
>
> Very informal: That was a difficult test!!!

9 End the sentences in the postcard below with a period, a question mark, or an exclamation point. Then discuss your choices with a partner.

Dear Chen,

I went to Marrakech on vacation .... Do you know where Marrakech is .... It's in Morocco .... It's a famous city, but it isn't the capital .... We went shopping, and we ate at some great Moroccan restaurants .... I bought a beautiful leather belt and some gold earrings .... Later, we took a trip to the desert .... I rode a camel .... It wasn't very comfortable, but it was interesting ....

Your friend,
Mike

Spelling review

10 Write the past tense of the verbs into the puzzle. Then read down to answer this question:

What city is this?

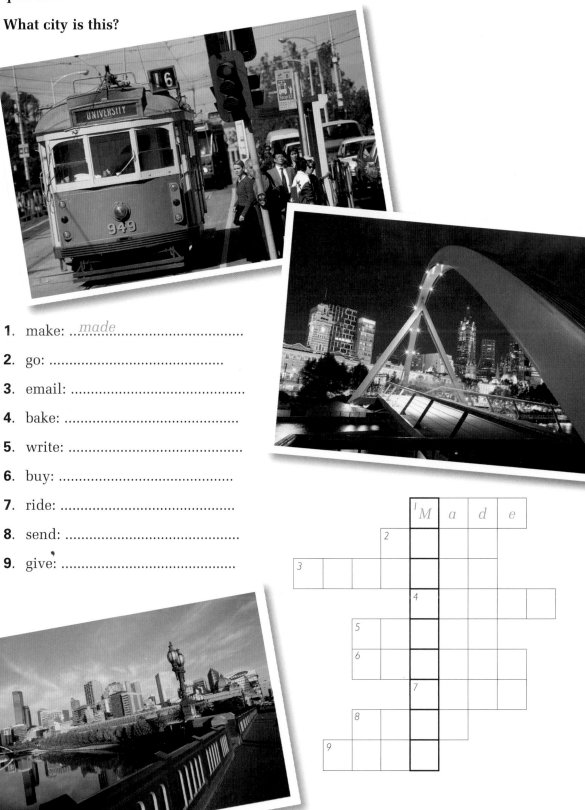

1. make: ...*made*...........................
2. go: ....
3. email: ....
4. bake: ....
5. write: ....
6. buy: ....
7. ride: ....
8. send: ....
9. give: ....

Put it together: A vacation postcard

a   You're on vacation! Choose one of the postcards below, find your own postcard, or draw your own picture.

b   Write some ideas for your postcard.

Who I'm writing to: ....

Will it be formal or informal? ....

Where I am: ....

What I'm doing: ....

What I did: ....

A question or exclamation: ....

c   Write your postcard on a separate sheet of paper. Include the name of the person you are writing to and your own name.

d   ⟳ Share your postcards. Put them on the walls of your classroom, or spread them on a desk or table. Cover your name, or fold the paper so that no one can read your name. Then read your classmates' postcards. Can you guess who wrote each one?

> I think that one's from Luisa!

> That postcard sounds like it's from Ken.

10 It's a kind of French game

In this unit, you will …

■ learn vocabulary to describe popular international items

■ learn when and how to use passive sentences

■ learn about the topic sentence, supporting sentences, and the concluding sentence

1 Work with a partner. Look at the vocabulary categories on the left. Then cross out the example that does not belong.

a.	clothing	dress	suit	~~cheese~~	hat
b.	game	chess	tiger	ping-pong	sudoku
c.	dessert	jazz	ice cream	cheesecake	chocolate
d.	food	curry	dumplings	salad	necklace
e.	toy	kite	yo-yo	rose	doll
f.	musical instrument	TV	piano	guitar	drum

2 Keep the same partner. What is the word that you crossed out? Take turns explaining.

Cheese is a kind of food.

3 Read the paragraphs below. Complete the description with a category word from exercise 1.

pétanque, France

hanbok, Korea

mochi, Japan

poi balls, New Zealand

Pétanque is a kind of French _____. Sometimes it is called boules. It is played in the park with metal balls. It's usually played by older people, but I like playing pétanque too!

The hanbok is a kind of Korean _____. It is worn on special occasions. Hanbok are very colorful. My hanbok has a blue skirt and a red blouse.

Mochi is a kind of Japanese _____. It is made from rice. It is used in many dishes. My favorite kind of mochi is sweet, and it is eaten for dessert.

Poi balls look like they are used for sports or games, but they are actually a kind of traditional _____. They make a sound when they are used. These days, they are used in dances and for exercise.

The passive

Active voice

subject	verb	object	prepositional phrase
My mother	made	cookies	with flour, eggs, butter, and sugar

Passive voice

subject (the object from an active sentence)	*be* + verb (participle)	prepositional phrase
Mochi	is made	from rice.
Varenyky	are eaten	in Ukraine and Russia.

You know that the most common pattern of an English sentence is

subject + verb + object

My mother   made   cookies.

In English, the first noun of the sentence is usually the most important. In the sentence above, we pay attention to the words "My mother."

However, sometimes you don't know the subject (who made the cookies), or you don't care. Then the passive is useful. The object is moved to the front of the sentence to become a new subject:

Cookies are made *with flour, eggs, butter, and sugar.*

The object of the first sentence (*cookies*) is now the subject. The original subject (*mother*) is not in the sentence. A prepositional phrase follows the verb.

It's also possible to use the passive to emphasize the object:

The best cookies are made *by my mother.*

Again, the object of the first sentence (*cookies*) is now the subject. The original subject (*my mother*) is part of a prepositional phrase that comes after the verb.

4 Work with a partner. Read the paragraphs on page 75 again. <u>Underline</u> the passive sentences.

Forming the passive

The passive is formed with a form of the *be* verb plus the participle of the main verb. (For a list of common participles, see page 103). Remember that the *be* verb will agree with the new subject in front of it:

Present   *Tigers **are found** in India.*
          *Jazz **is played** in that club.*

Past   *That dress **was worn** on special occasions.*
          *Traditional music **was played** at my wedding.*

5 Write the missing verb forms in the chart.

present	past	participle
a. eat	_____	eaten
b. _____	found	_____
c. _____	_____	made
d. play	_____	_____
e. _____	threw	thrown
f. use	_____	_____
g. wear	wore	_____

6 Complete the sentences with the correct form of the passive. Pay attention to singular, plural, present, and past.

a. Dominoes are a kind of tile. Many different games .... played with dominoes.

b. Dominoes .... made from plastic now.

c. Many years ago, dominoes .... made from animal bone.

d. A domino tile .... painted with black spots. Each side of the domino has a different number of spots.

e. The spots .... matched together when you play a game.

f. For example, a domino with three spots on one side .... matched with another domino with three spots on one side.

g. This kind of simple matching game .... played in my kindergarten. My classmates and I learned to count with this game.

h. Today, it .... enjoyed by many people in my country.

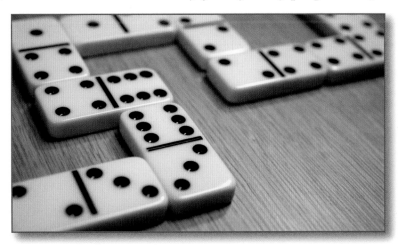

7 **Read the paragraph. Write the correct form of the verb (active or passive). Then compare your choices with a partner.**

> A boomerang is a kind of Australian toy. However, long ago,
> it was not a toy. It (use) _____ for
> hunting. The hunter (throw) _____ the
> boomerang at an animal, and it _____
> (kill) the animal. Boomerangs (make)
> _____ of wood, and sometimes
> they (paint) _____ with colorful designs.
> Now, boomerangs are popular with tourists. If you visit
> Australia, why don't you buy a boomerang as a souvenir?

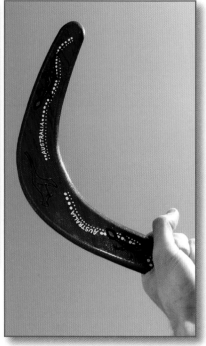

The topic sentence

You already know that a paragraph is a group of
sentences about one topic or idea. Many English
paragraphs—and all of the ones that you will write for school
assignments—include a **topic sentence**. This sentence tells the reader:

- your topic

- your idea or opinion about that topic, or an explanation of the topic

<u>My friend and I</u> <u>have had many similar experiences</u>.
    topic   idea

<u>Mochi</u> <u>is a kind of Japanese food</u>.
topic   explanation

The topic sentence is usually, but not always, the first sentence in the paragraph.

8 **Look at these topic sentences from paragraphs you have read in this book. Circle the topic, and <u>underline</u> the idea about the topic.**

a. <u>I'm studying</u> (art.)

b. I go to an unusual high school in Vermont.

c. I have a new sister!

d. You're an Aries.

e. I went to Marrakech on vacation.

f. Pétanque is a kind of French game.

Supporting sentences

After the topic sentence come the supporting sentences. These sentences can:

- explain the idea in the topic sentence
- give examples
- give reasons to prove your opinion
- tell a story

However, the supporting sentences must all be about the topic and the idea in the topic sentence.

9 **Work with a partner. Read the paragraph. Cross out any sentences that do not support the topic sentence.**

Varenyky are a kind of Ukrainian food. I went to Ukraine a few years ago. They are made from flour. Inside, they are stuffed with potatoes, cheese, and onions. I really like potatoes. They are seasoned with a little salt and pepper. Sometimes people make sweet *varenyky*. These are filled with fruit or berries and sugar. *Borchst* is a kind of Ukrainian soup. *Varenyky* are also eaten in Russia. You should try *varenyky*. They're really delicious.

10 **Work with a partner. Check (✓) the sentences that you could add to the paragraph in exercise 9 as support. Where would you add them?**

☐ Potatoes are not expensive in Ukraine.

☐ They look like dumplings.

☐ Many Ukrainian dishes taste good to me.

☐ They are served for dessert.

☐ I never cooked varenyky.

The concluding sentence

The last sentence in a paragraph is often a concluding sentence. This sentence can:

- repeat the idea of the topic sentence
- offer a final comment on the topic

Not all paragraphs have concluding sentences. The writer chooses whether to finish with a concluding sentence or not.

11 Work with a partner. Read some paragraphs from previous units again. Do they have a concluding sentence?

a. Unit 1, exercise 6, page 11   ☐ yes   ☐ no

b. Unit 4, exercise 7, page 34   ☐ yes   ☐ no

c. Unit 5, exercise 7, page 40   ☐ yes   ☐ no

d. Unit 5, exercise 8, page 40   ☐ yes   ☐ no

e. Unit 8, exercise 1, Emma, page 60   ☐ yes   ☐ no

f. Unit 9, exercise 9, page 72   ☐ yes   ☐ no

12 Read the paragraph. Then check (✓) the best concluding sentence. Discuss your choice with a partner.

> Mah jongg is a kind of Chinese game. It's played with tiles and dice. It's usually played by four people. It's not difficult to learn, but you need skill to win. You also need luck! These days, you can even play mah jongg on the computer.

a. ☐ It's more difficult than chess.

b. ☐ Mah jongg is popular all over the world now.

c. ☐ I usually lose.

13 Work with a partner. Below are sentences from a paragraph.

a Number them in the correct order. Write 1 by the first sentence, 2 by the second sentence, etc.

b Then write them into a paragraph. Use good paragraph form.

.... First, the beef, cheese, and vegetables are put inside taco shells.
.... Salsa is a spicy tomato sauce.
.... Tacos are a kind of Mexican food.
.... Then they are served with salsa.
.... They are delicious!
.... They are made with beef, cheese, and vegetables.
.... They look a little like a sandwich.

....
....
....
....
....

c Now compare your paragraph with another pair. Did you choose the same order?

Spelling review

14 Write the missing letters.

a. ___ ___ ss ___ ___ ___   This is eaten after dinner.

b. ___ ___ zz   A kind of music

c. ___ ___ rr ___   A spicy sauce

d. ___ ___ ee ___ ___   It's made from milk.

e. ___ oo ___ ___ ___ ___   A kind of sweet snack

f. ___ ___ ___ ss   A kind of clothing for women

g. ___ ___ ff ___ ___ ___ ___ ___   Not easy

h. ___ ___ pp ___ ___   A black spice

i. ___ oo ___ ___ ___ ___ ___ ___   An Australian toy

j. ___ ___ ___ ll   You need this to win at chess.

Put it together: International fair

a Choose something from your own country or a country that interests you. Write your ideas about it in the word map.

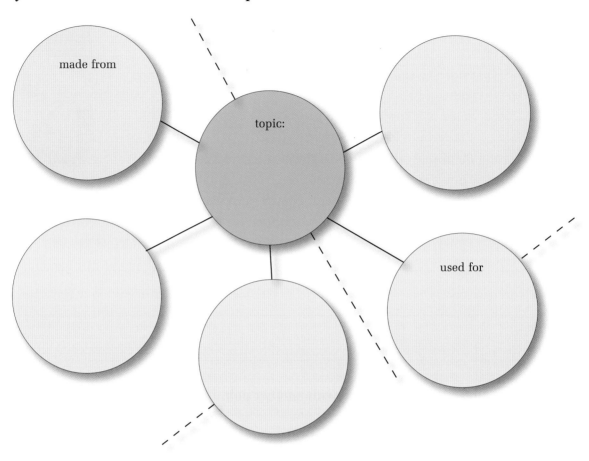

made from

topic:

used for

b What do you want to say about your topic? Write your topic sentence here:

....

c Write a concluding sentence here:

....

d Write your paragraph on a separate sheet of paper.

e 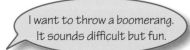 Share your ideas. Post your paragraphs on the walls of your classroom or spread them on a table or desk. Read your classmates' paragraphs. Then tell the class about something you want to see, do, or try.

> I want to throw a boomerang.
> It sounds difficult but fun.

> I want to try dumplings.
> They sound delicious!

▮▮ It has great graphics

In this unit, you will ...
- ▮ learn vocabulary to describe popular media
- ▮ add supporting sentences and concluding sentences
- ▮ learn to strengthen and weaken adjectives
- ▮ learn to use *too* and *not ... enough*

I Read the different reviews of a video game. Who liked the game? Who didn't like it?

★★★★☆ AAAGamer	I think Omega Chronicles is a wonderful game. It's an action-adventure game for teens and adults. It has great graphics and really interesting gameplay. The characters are realistic. I recommend this game.
★☆☆☆☆ Dark Lord	I didn't like this game. It's too difficult, and the directions aren't clear enough. The soundtrack was quite good, but it was too loud.
★★★★★ Angelady	This game is cool! I love the special effects. You can play by yourself or with a friend. The puzzles are very challenging, but they aren't too difficult. Buy or rent this game! You will enjoy it.
★★★★★ Time Knight	Omega Chronicles is really fun. The action is fast, the plot is amazing, and the gameplay is realistic. It's kind of expensive, but I recommend it. It's a great game.

2 Work with a partner. Read the sentences. Circle T if the sentence is true. Circle F if the sentence is false.

    a. *AAAGamer* thinks the game is for children.   T   F

    b. *Dark Lord* thinks the game isn't easy enough.   T   F

    c. *Dark Lord* didn't like the soundtrack.   T   F

    d. *Angelady* thinks the puzzles are difficult.   T   F

    e. *Time Knight* likes the game.   T   F

    f. *Time Knight* thinks the game is expensive.   T   F

3 Work with a partner. Write these adjectives into the correct place in the chart below. Can you think of other positive and negative adjectives to describe a video game?

> ✓amazing   challenging   childish   clear   difficult   disappointing   expensive   fun   great   interesting   realistic   wonderful

positive	negative
amazing	

4 Work with a partner. Complete the word map below with words from the box and your own ideas. Some words can be used for more than one category.

> actor   beat   character   gameplay   graphics   lyrics   plot   sound effects   soundtrack   special effects   vocals   writing

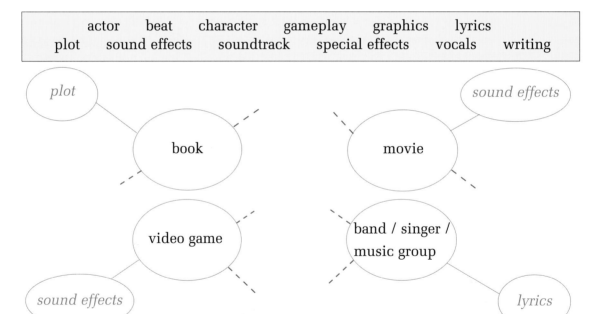

5 Complete the sentences with the name of a book, movie, video game, group or singer. Then share your sentences with a partner. Were any of your sentences about the same thing?

a. .... has a boring plot.

b. I liked the special effects in ....

c. .... has/have great vocals.

d. I didn't notice the sound effects in ....

e. My favorite character in .... is ....

6a Work with a partner. Choose a movie, book, singer or musical group, or video game. Write sentences about it, but do not write its name.

....

....

....

....

....

....

....

....

....

b Now join another pair and read your sentences. Can they guess its name?

There are four movies
in this series.
The actors are very famous.

Is it *Lord of the Rings?*

No, I'm sorry.

The special effects are amazing.
The main character is a pirate.

Is it *Pirates of the Caribbean?*

Yes, that's right!.

Adding support

The paragraphs in this unit describe what something is like—what it looks like, what it sounds like, what the experience is like.

The topic sentence names what you are describing (a book; a movie) and your opinion about it (you liked it; you think it's terrible).

The supporting sentences add details and examples about your topic that explain your opinion.

7 **Read the topic sentences. Then check (✓) the sentences you think support the topic sentence. Discuss your choices with a partner.**

a *Pirates of the Caribbean* is an excellent movie series.

☐ The movies are based on a ride at Disneyland.

☐ The actors are terrific. I especially like Johnny Depp.

☐ I have the first movie on DVD.

☐ The stories are not realistic, but they are interesting.

☐ The costumes and soundtrack are great, too.

☐ Some of Johnny Depp's other movies are a little strange.

☐ They are action movies, but there is humor and romance, too.

b I think *Moby Dick* is a boring book.

☐ It is too long.

☐ I can't understand all of the old-fashioned language.

☐ I'm not interested in the sea or fishing.

☐ I never saw the movie of *Moby Dick*.

☐ The plot moves really slowly.

☐ I don't like the characters.

☐ Actually, I'm not very interested in reading.

☐ There is too much description and not enough action.

8 **Write a concluding sentence for each paragraph in exercise 7. Then compare your sentences with a partner or group.**

....

....

Strengthening and weakening adjectives

Here are some words and phrases to make your adjectives stronger or weaker:

stronger	weaker
very	a little
really	a bit
quite	kind of
extremely	somewhat

Use these expressions before the adjective:

The plot was strange.
*The plot was **quite** strange.*   = more strange
*The plot was **somewhat** strange.*   = less strange

These expressions are common after the verbs *be* and *have*.

9 **Underline the expressions from the chart that are used in the reviews on page 83.**

10 **Rewrite the sentences with the expressions in parentheses.**
  a. I think animated movies are interesting, so I like *Princess Mononoke*. (very)
  I think animated movies are very interesting, so I like "Princess Mononoke."
  b. The movie is old. (kind of) ....
  c. It is still good. (quite) ....
  d. The plot is confusing. (somewhat) ....
  e. The animation is amazing. (really) ....

Stand-alone adjectives

Some adjectives are not usually strengthened or weakened because they are already very strong or weak: *best, worst, unique, favorite, only*

11 **Work with a partner. Read the sentences. Strengthen, weaken, or add nothing to the underlined adjective. Then compare your ideas with another pair.**

  a. I like this book, but the vocabulary is ^very difficult.

  b. *Harry Potter* is the top children's book.

  c. The words to this song are childish, but I still like it.

  d. *Shadow of the Colossus* is my favorite video game.

  e. A-mei has a beautiful voice.

12 Work with a partner. Rewrite the following paragraph. Add four expressions to strengthen and weaken some of the adjectives. Then share your new paragraph with another pair.

> *Krazy 4 English is my favorite new group. Their songs have funny lyrics and a strong beat. Their guitar player is amazing, too. Their best single, "Luv 2 Take Tests," has a nice melody. I like to sing it. I'm shy, so I sing it alone in my room. Krazy 4 English are popular now, but I think they will be more popular in the future.*

....

....

....

....

....

too and *not* ... *enough*

Here is another way to strengthen or weaken an adjective that means you are criticizing something:

The gameplay is difficult.

The gampelay is too difficult.   = more difficult

The gameplay isn't difficult enough.   = less difficult

13 Rewrite the sentences below. Add *too* for the sentences marked ⤴. And *not ... enough* to the sentences marked ⤵.

I don't like Krazy 4 English.

a. ⤴ I think they're popular. *I think they're too popular.* ....

b. ⤴ Their songs are short. ....

c. ⤴ The lead singer is strange. ....

d. ⤵ The words are clear. ....

e. ⤴ Their top song is childish. ....

f. ⤵ The vocals are loud. ....

g. ⤵ The beat is clear. ....

h. ⤴ Their concert tickets are expensive. ....

14 Unscramble the sentences.

a. is / movie / that / long / too

....

b. interesting / enough / the / effects / special / aren't

....

c. too / the gameplay / challenging / is / a little bit

....

d. extremely / the / is / exciting / soundtrack

....

e. enough / the / realistic / isn't / plot

....

f. somewhat / is / beat / slow / the

....

g. long and / is too / boring / the book / too

....

h. effects / really / are / the / cool / sound

....

Spelling review

15 **One word in each sentence is spelled incorrectly. Cross it out and correct the spelling.**

a. *Stormbreaker* is an ~~extremly~~ *extremely* good book.

b. The main caracter is a high school boy. His name is Alex Rider.

c. It's an action-adventere book, and it's for teens and adults.

d. The plot is somwhat unrealistic, but it's exciting.

e. The writing is quiet good, and it's funny too.

f. A movie was made from this book, but it wasn't good enouff.

g. It was kind of disapointing, but it had good special effects.

h. I didn't enjoy the movie, but I reccomend the book.

Put it together: A media review

a Choose a book, movie, band, video game, or something similar to review. You can choose something you recommend–or something you *don't* recommend! Complete the word map below with your ideas.

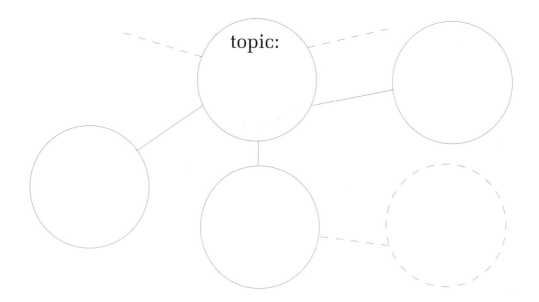

topic:

b What do you want to say about your topic? Write your topic sentence here:

....

c Do you want to have a concluding sentence? If so, write it here:

....

d Write your paragraph on a separate sheet of paper.

e Share your reviews. Post your paragraphs on the walls of your classroom or spread them on a table or desk. Read your classmates' reviews. Then tell the class about one or two things you learned about that you'd like to experience, and why.

I want to see Howl's Moving Castle. It sounds really interesting.

I want to read Twilight. My best friend also likes it.

12 *I've never been to Australia*

In this unit, you will …

- ■ learn vocabulary for writing about travel and experiences
- ■ learn and practice the present perfect tense
- ■ contrast the present perfect and the simple past
- ■ use *However* in a paragraph

1 Write the verbs under the correct pictures.

✓ fly	go	hold	see	travel	visit

a. *fly* in an airplane Sam ☐ Writer ☐	**b.** _____ to a foreign country Sam ☐ Writer ☐	**c.** _____ Australia Sam ☐ Writer ☐
d. _____ kangaroos Sam ☐ Writer ☐	**e.** _____ a koala Sam ☐ Writer ☐	**f.** _____ surfing Sam ☐ Writer ☐

2 Read the paragraph below. Check (✓) the activities in exercise 1 that Sam did and then check (✓) the activities that the writer has done.

> I envy my friend Sam. He's traveled to many foreign countries. Last year, he flew to Australia. He saw kangaroos, and he held a koala. He went to the beach and went surfing. I've never been to a foreign country. I've never flown in an airplane. I've seen kangaroos and koalas, but I saw them in a zoo. I've been to the beach, but I've never gone surfing. Sam has had more interesting experiences than I have.

The present perfect

This tense is called the "present" perfect, but we use it to talk about things that happened in the past. It is one of the most common tenses in written English.

Noun	verb: *have* + present participle		noun (direct object)	preposition + noun (adverb phrase)
Sam He	has hasn't has never	seen been	kangaroos.	to Australia.
We	have haven't have never	flown		in an airplane.

Use the *present perfect:*

*   to describe a life experience:
    *Sam **has seen** a kangaroo.*
    *I**'ve** never **been** to Australia.*

*   to describe something you've done in the past more than once:
    *I**'ve seen** "Star Wars" eleven times.*
    *I**'ve played** that game a lot.*

*   to talk about something that started in the past, and is still true now:
    *I**'ve lived** here for three years.*
    *Nina **has played** the piano for a long time.*

Form the present perfect with the present tense of *have* + the past participle.

Remember: *have* must agree with the subject.

(See page 103 for a list of common irregular past participles).

3 **Write the past participle of the following verbs.**

a. have: I have ......*had*............ many interesting experiences.

b. travel: I have .... to several countries.

c. take: I have .... many photographs.

d. eat: On vacation, I have .... a lot of delicious food.

e. see: I haven't .... every country.

f. be: For example, I've never .... to Kenya.

4   **Write the verb in the present perfect. Make sure that *has* and *have* agree with the subject.**

   a. My parents .... (be) to many interesting places.

   b. My father .... (travel) to Switzerland and Austria.

   c. He loves mountains, so he .... (see) the Alps many times.

   d. My mother likes swimming. She .... (take) diving trips to
   Guam and Saipan.

   e. I .... never .... (visit) a foreign country,
   but my parents .... (tell) me about their travels many times.

Contrast with the simple past

Use the *simple past:*

- to describe an action that happened once in the past:
  *Sam **saw** a kangaroo last year.*
  *I **went** to China.*

- to describe an action that had a clear start and finish, and is finished now:
  *I **drove** to school.*
  *I **ate** lunch at 12:00.*

Use the **simple past** with expressions such as *at 3:00, yesterday, on Monday, last year, this morning*:
  *I **got up** at 6:00.*
  *I **had** a piano lesson on Tuesday.*

Use the **present perfect** with adverbs such as *already, never, ever, yet, for, since*:
  ***Have** you ever **gone** surfing?*
  *I've never **traveled**.*
  *I've **known** my best friend since elementary school.*

5   **Work with a partner. <u>Underline</u> the sentences on page 91 that use the present perfect. <u>Double <u>underline</u></u> the sentences that use the simple past. For each sentence, explain why the present perfect or simple past was used with one of the reasons below:**

present perfect	simple past
• It's talking about his life experience. • It's talking about something he did more than one time in the past.	• It's talking about something he did only one time in the past.

6 Answer the questions with information from exercise 2 on page 91. Use short answers (*Yes, he has; Yes, they have; No, he hasn't; No, they haven't*).

a. Has Sam flown in an airplane? ....

b. Has Sam held a koala? ....

c. Has the writer visited Australia? ....

d. Have Sam and the writer seen kangaroos? ....

e. Has the writer been to the beach? ....

f. Has the writer gone surfing? ....

7 Look at the activities in exercise 6. Have you done those activities once, many times, or never? Write sentences. Follow the example.

I flew in an airplane last year. Or, *I've flown in an airplane many times.*

a. ....

b. ....

c. ....

d. ....

e. ....

f. ....

8 Read the following paragraph. Write the correct form of the verb in parentheses.

My friend Amy and I (have) _____ many similar experiences. We both (live) _____ in this town all our lives. We (go) _____ to the same elementary school and middle school, and now we're in the same high school. Amy and I (study) _____ musical instruments for several years. She plays the piano and I play the violin. Amy (travel) _____ to Kaohsiung, and I (visit) _____ Hong Kong. We (not / be) _____ to Europe or South America, but we both want to go. We are different people, but we (have) _____ similar lives so far.

9 Write five questions for a partner using the present perfect and, in case your partner answers "yes," the past tense. Use a separate sheet of paper and follow the example.

Have you ever been to New York? When did you go?
....

10 Interview your partner. Then use your partner's answers to write a paragraph about you and your partner like the one on page 94. Use a separate sheet of paper, and begin with one of these sentences:

My classmate (_____) *and I have had many similar experiences.*

My classmate (_____) *and I haven't had many similar experiences.*

However

You already know how to use *but* in a sentence to show contrasting information:

I've been to Australia, **but** *I haven't been to New Zealand.*

However has a similar meaning. It is used at the beginning of a sentence to show that the next sentence, or even the next section of the paragraph, is different from what came before:

I've been to Australia, New Zealand, and Tahiti. **However,** *I haven't been to many cities in my own country.*

11 Draw a line to match the sentences on the left with the sentences on the right.

a. I've eaten Mexican food.	**1**. However, I've never been to Paris.
b. I haven't ridden a camel.	**2**. However, I've tried windsurfing.
c. I've been to France.	**3**. However, I've ridden a horse several times.
d. I've never been to India.	
e. I've gone skiing.	**4**. However, I've never tried snowboarding.
f. I've never gone surfing.	**5**. However, I've never cooked it.
	6. However, I've eaten Indian food.

12 Read the following paragraph. Where would you put the word *However*? Discuss your choice with a partner.

I'm still in high school, but I think I've done many interesting things. I haven't traveled much, and I haven't been to a foreign country.
a) _____ I haven't ridden a horse or a camel, and I haven't seen many famous places.
b) _____ I've ridden my bicycle all around my city. I've taken a lot of interesting photos, and I've met a lot of people. I've played a lot of sports, like basketball, soccer, and tennis. I've had several part-time jobs, and I learned a lot about working. c) _____ I want to do many more things in my life, but I think I've already done a lot.

13 Read the following sentences. Check (✓) the sentences that tell about the foods the person has tried. Write an (✗) by the foods the person hasn't tried.

___✓___ I've tried Indian food.

_____ I can cook some Chinese dishes, too.

_____ I've never eaten French food.

_____ I've cooked a lot of Italian food.

_____ I made spaghetti last week.

_____ I haven't tried Korean food.

_____ I've eaten a lot of Chinese dishes.

_____ I'm interested in Spanish food, but I haven't tried any yet.

14 Work with a partner. Use the information in exercise 13 to write about the foods the person has tried. Then use *However* and write about the foods the person hasn't tried.

I'm very interested in international food. I've tried a lot of different kinds of

food, but there are some kinds I haven't tried yet. ....

....

....

....

....

There are still many kinds of food I want to try.

Spelling review

15 Look at the chart with examples of how participles are spelled. Then write the verbs below into the correct column.

regular: add ~ed/d	double the last letter and add ~ed	drop the ~y and add ~ied	irregular
visit → visited	stop → stopped	hurry → hurried	go → gone

eat	live	shop	try	wear
do	plan	stay	want	worry

Put it together: My story so far

a What have you done in your life so far? What haven't you done yet? Make a list. Follow the examples.

places	activities	foods	sights	subjects
I've been to (Dubai).	*I've (gone surfing).*	*I've tried (coconut).*	*I've seen …*	*I've studied …*
I haven't / I've never been to (Brazil).	*I haven't …*	*I've never eaten (snake).*	*I've never seen …*	*I've never learned …*

b Choose one of these topic sentences to begin your paragraph.

> *I've lived for _____ years, but I haven't experienced many things yet.*

(Write first about the things you have done. Then use *However* and write about the things you haven't done.)

> I've lived for _____ years, and I've already experienced many things.

(Write first about the things you haven't done. Then use *However* and write about the things you have done.)

c Write your paragraph on a separate sheet of paper.

d ☐ Share your story with a small group. Read your paragraph to the group. Talk about experiences you've all had that are similar, and what experiences only one of you has had.

Key sentence patterns

The verb *be* (Unit 3)

Subject (noun / pronoun)	verb *be*	noun, adjective, or prepositional phrase (adverb)
I	am	Thai.
My friends and I	are	hungry.
My hometown	is	in the mountains.

Stative verbs (Unit 4)

Subject	stative verb	adjective
You	seem	friendly.
My teacher	looks	happy.

Action verbs with objects (Unit 6)

Subject	verb	noun (direct object)	prepositional phrase
I	play	soccer	in the park.
Kiyo	takes	piano lessons	

Action verbs with direct and indirect objects (Unit 9)

Subject	verb	noun (direct object)	(preposition) + noun (indirect object)
I	wrote	a letter	to Charlie.
You	gave	some money	to me.

Subject	verb	noun (indirect object)	noun (direct object)
I	wrote	Charlie	a letter.
You	gave	me	some money.

The passive (Unit 10)

Subject (the object from an active sentence)	*be* + verb (participle)	prepositional phrase
Mochi	is made	from rice.
Tigers	are found	in India.

Regular verbs

PRESENT TENSE

Affirmative Statements

I like You like He likes She likes It likes We like They like	school.

Negative Statements

I do You do He does She does It does We do They do	not like	school.

Yes / No Questions

Do I Do you Does he Does she Does it Do we Do they	like	school?

Short Answers

affirmative	negative
Yes, I do.	No, I don't.
Yes, you do.	No, you don't.
Yes, he does.	No, he doesn't.
Yes, she does.	No, she doesn't.
Yes, it does.	No, it doesn't.
Yes, we do.	No, we don't.
Yes, they do.	No, they don't.

PAST TENSE

Affirmative Statements

I You He She It We They	liked	school.

Negative Statements

I You He She It We They	did not like	school.

Yes / No Questions

Did	I you he she it we they	like	school?

Short Answers

affirmative	negative
Yes, I did.	No, I didn't.
Yes, you did.	No, you didn't.
Yes, he did.	No, he didn't.
Yes, she did.	No, she didn't.
Yes, it did.	No, it didn't.
Yes, we did.	No, we didn't.
Yes, they did.	No, they didn't.

Can

PRESENT TENSE

Affirmative Statements

I You He She It We They	can	speak	English.

Negative Statements

I You He She It We They	can not	speak	English.

Yes / No **Questions**

Can	I you he she it we they	speak	Swedish?

Short Answers

affirmative			**negative**		
Yes,	I you he she it we they	can.	No,	I you he she it we they	can't.

PAST TENSE
Affirmative Statements

I You He She It We They	could	play	the piano.

Negative Statements

I You He She It We They	could not	play	the piano.

Yes / No Questions

Could	I you he she it we they	play	the piano?

Short Answers

affirmative			negative		
Yes,	I you he she it we they	could.	No,	I you he she it we they	couldn't.

Common irregular verbs

Here is a list of common irregular verbs in English with their past tense (*I took the test*) and past participle (*I have taken three tests this month*).

Infinitive	Simple past	Past participle	Infinitive	Simple past	Past participle
be	was/were	been	make	made	made
become	became	become	meet	met	met
begin	began	begun	pay	paid	paid
break	broke	broken	put	put	put
bring	brought	brought	read	read	read
buy	bought	bought	ride	rode	ridden
catch	caught	caught	run	ran	run
choose	chose	chosen	say	said	said
come	came	come	see	saw	seen
cost	cost	cost	sell	sold	sold
cut	cut	cut	send	sent	sent
do	did	done	show	showed	shown
draw	drew	drawn	sing	sang	sung
drink	drank	drunk	sit	sat	sat
drive	drove	driven	sleep	slept	slept
eat	ate	eaten	speak	spoke	spoken
fall	fell	fallen	spend	spent	spent
feel	felt	felt	stand	stood	stood
find	found	found	swim	swam	swum
fly	flew	flown	take	took	taken
forget	forgot	forgotten	teach	taught	taught
get	got	gotten	tell	told	told
give	gave	given	think	thought	thought
go	went	gone	throw	threw	thrown
have	had	had	understand	understood	understood
hear	heard	heard	wear	wore	worn
know	knew	known	win	won	won
leave	left	left	write	wrote	written
lose	lost	lost			

Macmillan Education
Between Towns Road, Oxford OX4 3PP
A division of Macmillan Publishers Limited

Companies and representatives throughout the world

ISBN 978-0-230-41591-1

Designed by xen
Illustrated by John Graham, Ciaran Hughes,
Will Mitchell and Vicky Woodgate
Cover design by xen based on a design by Jackie Hill at
320 Design
Cover illustration/photograph by xen

Authors' acknowledgements
Thanks to Mary Ann Maynard and Kristopher Bayne
who provided valuable input on early drafts of the
original manuscript. Finally, I gratefully acknowledge
the love and support of my family, Will and Sebastian
Mitchell. A special tip of the hat to Sebastian for
contributing the title and some of the content for Unit
11.

The publishers would like to thank (in alphabetical
order):
Jim Chou, Kevin Cleary, Concordia Language Villages,
Kyung-seo Koo, Jessie Liao, Michael McCollister, Lesley
Riley, Glen Swafford, Linda Szu-wei Wu, Yi-ling Wu.

The authors and publishers would like to thank
the following for permission to reproduce their
photographs:
Alamy pp7 (t), 11, 22(l), 24, 37(tr, bl), 41(t), 73(t), 75(l),
79, 95 Inspirestock Inc p52(t);
Bananastock pp25 (l, r), 60(mr, ml, b), 78;
Corbis pp32, 52(m, b), 55, 74(l), 75(lm), 80;
Digital Vision p32;
Getty pp8 (l, r), 30, 39, 52(t), 60(t), 60(br), 73(m), 74(r),
75(rm) Steve Casimiro p72, Emmanuel Foure p52(c);
NASA p18;
Photodisc pp37 (tl), 41(m), 44, 60, 72, 73(b), 74(c), 77,
81;
Photolibrary/Agestock p52(b);
Rex W.Disney/Everett p86;
Superstock pp7 (bl, br), 11(r), 25(c), 37(br), 39, 41(b),
68, 75(r).

Printed and bound in Thailand

2015 2014 2013 2012 2011
10 9 8 7 6 5 4 3 2 1